# STUDIES IN STATECRAFT

# STUDIES IN STATECRAFT

BEING CHAPTERS, BIOGRAPHICAL AND
BIBLIOGRAPHICAL, MAINLY ON THE
SIXTEENTH CENTURY

BY

SIR GEOFFREY BUTLER, K.B.E., M.A.

KENNIKAT PRESS
Port Washington, N. Y./London

STUDIES IN STATECRAFT

First published in 1920
Reissued in 1970 by Kennikat Press
Library of Congress Catalog Card No: 79-110899
SBN 8046-0882-2

Manufactured by Taylor Publishing Company    Dallas, Texas

TO

MONSIEUR ANDRÉ TARDIEU,

AUTHOR, STATESMAN, DIPLOMAT,
THESE ESSAYS AND NOTES,
MOSTLY UPON THE HISTORY OF FRENCH THOUGHT,
ARE DEDICATED,
IN RECOLLECTION OF
HAPPY FRANCO-BRITISH COOPERATION
IN THE PAST,
PARTICULARLY OURS IN THE UNITED STATES
1917—1919.

# PREFACE

"An ounce of example is worth a ton of theory" (SURTEES).

THESE essays make but the humblest of pretensions. Material for their composition was gathered when, with my pupils at Corpus, I was pursuing the subject of the development of European history in the XV and XVI centuries. Recent events have kindled general interest in the history of international relations and of the theories which have governed them. Since Wheaton, now nearly a century ago, wrote his famous and useful book the treatment of the subject has outgrown the capacity of any one writer. The field to be covered is vast and the maps are not good: to complete even a preliminary survey there is need of cooperation between students. If these chapters have any value, it will be in that they can save a fellow student trouble in connection with a certain area hitherto not exhaustively explored. Certainly these sketches are far from exhausting it. The various studies, biographical and bibliographical, are consecutive only in the sense that we were following through two crucial centuries the process by which men came to realise that a new political conception—the nation state—had found embodiment, and those by which they grasped that the relation which these nation states bore to each other brought with it certain logical results. It is a sphere covered by the most able of modern historians, jurists and philosophers.

Man, since the Renaissance, has remained at heart the same. It is not therefore novel ideas that are to be expected in these pages. Pacificism, "Weltmacht," internationalism, diplomacy based upon ideals—all were ideas familiar to the men of these two centuries, as they are to us still, but four or five hundred years ago men were poorer in generic terms than we are, and, as the labels are missing, the facts are sometimes overlooked.

I have been inconsistent in leaving my quoted passages in the second chapter untranslated. As the interest of this chapter is far more technical than any of the others, I have thought it best to do so. The reader who prefers them will find an English translation at the end of the book in Appendix C.

My thanks are due to the publishers and editors of the *Edinburgh Review*, the *English Historical Review* and the *XIX Century and After* for permission to reproduce from articles which appeared in their pages.

My wife helped me to read the proofs. Mr Stephen Gaselee, Librarian to H.M. Foreign Office, showed great kindness in reading them also. To them, to Professor W. W. Buckland and to Mr G. T. Lapsley, among others, I owe a deep debt of obligation, which must not involve them in responsibility for any of the more serious mistakes of treatment which my readers may discover. For these the responsibility is mine.

GEOFFREY BUTLER.

Corpus Christi College,
Cambridge.
1 *October* 1920.

# TABLE OF CONTENTS

|  | PAGE |
|---|---|
| PREFACE . . . . . . . . . | v |

CHAP.

| I. BISHOP RODERICK AND RENAISSANCE PACIFICISM . . . . . . . . . | 1 |
|---|---|
| II. THE FRENCH "CIVILIANS," ROMAN LAW AND THE NEW MONARCHY . . . . . | 26 |
| III. WILLIAM POSTEL, WORLD PEACE THROUGH WORLD POWER . . . . . . | 38 |
| IV. SULLY AND HIS GRAND DESIGN . . . | 65 |
| V. "THE GRAND DESIGN" OF EMERICH CRUCÉ | 91 |

APPENDICES

| A. PASSAGES QUOTED IN CHAPTER I . . | 105 |
|---|---|
| B. A BIBLIOGRAPHY OF RODERICUS SANCIUS | 108 |
| C. ENGLISH VERSION OF PASSAGES QUOTED IN CHAPTER II . . . . . . | 114 |
| D. A BIBLIOGRAPHY OF WILLIAM POSTEL . | 117 |
| CHRONOLOGICAL TABLE . . . . . . | 133 |
| INDEX . . . . . . . . . . | 135 |

# CHAPTER I

BISHOP RODERICK AND RENAISSANCE PACIFICISM

AMONG the manuscripts which form the princely gift of Archbishop Parker to the Library at Corpus Christi College, Cambridge, is one[1] whose contents may justly claim attention from the historian of the Law of Nations. Written, in a Roman hand of the fifteenth century, on vellum, it is a copy of a manuscript[2] in the Vatican Library, which still exists in the binding in which it was presented to Pope Paul II. How the Cambridge copy came into the hands of Parker is uncertain. It may have been a Canterbury book, one of those perhaps brought back by Prior Sellinge[3] to the Christ Church Priory, on the occasion of the Italian visit upon which Thomas Linacre was his companion. Even if this were so, there are indications that the Corpus book had other owners[4]. Data no longer exist for forming an incontrovertible opinion.

The manuscript contains among other historical documents of value[5] a dialogue upon the nature of

[1] No. 166.
[2] Vat. 4881. See Antonio, *Bibl. Hisp. vet.* under the author's name; Vairani, *Cremonensium monumenta*, p. 67.
[3] James, *Ancient Libraries of Canterbury and Dover*, p. l. Prior Sellinge was Prior of Christ Church 1472 to 1494.
[4] On several pages occurs the name Thomas Godsalve of Norwich, notary, sometime of Lichfield. On August 20, 1567, it belonged to Peter Hubbard (hobard) of Dennington. On the last flyleaf is fixed a piece of parchment with the following written upon it "henry blower re of...wax chandelour in S. Margetmoyses parishe in fridaye strete." Parker died in 1574.
[5] Creighton (*History of the Papacy*, Vol. III, p. 276) reproduces some of these. An error gives the number of the Corpus MS. as 161.

peace and war. It was written during the papacy of Paul II (1464–1471)[1]. Any discussion of this subject in past ages is likely to interest those who know how strong an influence mere hatred of war has had upon the growth of international law and organisation. But the epoch at which this dialogue was written gives it added point. The mediaeval world was passing into the modern world and of this process Italy was to see the first fruits. Into the unities of religion, language and social order, unbroken throughout Europe in the Middle Ages, men felt the imminent irruption of new categories, national churches, national literatures, the nation state. The symptoms were to spread and to become more clearly recognisable when (not in the religious sphere alone) the time was ripe for men to square their actions with their logic. In 1470, even in Italy, that time had not yet come and about the writings of this period there is an air of incompleteness. Largely this is due to the fact that those who wrote both incompletely grasped the point which was to be at issue and also employed to express themselves a terminology that was fast growing out of date. When the Spaniards first flooded Europe with silver from the Indies, statesmen and philosophers were not equipped with the mental machinery to meet the conditions to which the glut had led, until an inherited vocabulary had yielded way to those words and phrases which we can now see are fundamental to a theory of exchange. So it was with all the problems which the passing of the Middle Ages was to bring upon the world, not least the question of the relation between states, the theory of war and peace.

[1] It is dedicated to the Pope's nephew the Cardinal Marco Barbo, Bishop of Vicenza.

The author of the dialogue which is here under discussion, was in his own day a man of great literary prominence. Rodericus Sancius of Arevalo, who was born in 1404 and died in 1471, was well known in his own Spain successively as student, then doctor of laws of Salamanca, archdeacon of Burgos and finally Bishop of Zamora. He was more however than an ecclesiastical administrator. At an early age he was well seen at court and may be said to have joined the diplomatic service of King John II of Castille. He acted as his representative on missions to the Emperor, the Pope Eugenius IV then at Basel, to the French, the Milanese and the Burgundian courts. These journeys won for him European reputation and Pope Pius II brought him finally to Italy and within the circle of the Curia. In the complicated transactions in which the reign of Aeneas Sylvius Piccolomini abounded the pen of Rodericus was always at the service of his master up to the day on which, at Ancona, the dying Pontiff saw his well-meant efforts to lead a new crusade against the Turk were doomed to failure.

The new Pope Peter Barbo, Paul II, inherited a situation in which, even at the seat of government, Rome itself, lawlessness and discord were predominant. The Duke of Amalfi, alleging an unpaid debt of thirty thousand ducats, had occupied the Papal fortresses of Ostia, Spoleto and Tivoli, together with the castle of St Angelo. It needed a full fortnight's negotiation to dislodge him and, profiting perhaps from this humiliating experience, the Pope determined, in the selection of his fortress officers, that ability and discretion should weigh with him as well as congeniality or kinship. The day St Angelo was handed over Rodericus was appointed its castellan and the services which he had rendered the last Pope were continued to his successor.

Without a doubt the successor had every need of help and help in particular from men of brain. As we look back it is possible for us to see that the vital event of the period was the steady progress of the Turks, which had added to the capture of Constantinople the overrunning of the Balkan peninsula and the formation of an Eastern question still the bugbear of our diplomats. It was characteristic of the mind of Pius II that he should be the first of those who have suggested for the solution of that question a policy based upon "heroics." He loved the righteousness which looked to the mediaeval conception of a Christian Europe led by the successor of St Peter, he hated the iniquity behind the divisions and the selfishness which prevented the translation of that conception into fact; accordingly he died in the spiritual and political exile of Ancona. His life and his death provided a warning to all thinking statesmen; and Paul was not the statesman to neglect it.

The failure of Pius in his eyes was not one of misdirected aims but faulty methods. He had tried to sail the ship of state against the wind. It might seem to be a longer process but none the less it was quicker far to tack. To continue the metaphor it might be desirable to overhaul the ship before the voyage was attempted. The pontificate of Paul II, therefore, is one in which a Turkish policy but indirectly figures. His defenders, and they are many and convincing[1], explain his concentration upon the reform of the Curia,

[1] See for instance Pastor, *History of the Popes* (edition by Antrobus), Vol. IV, *passim*.

his efforts to adopt sound plans for Papal action in Italy, as well as in other European countries, as the fruit of his conviction as to the necessity of a period of preparation. It was a case of drawing back and of retrenchment in order later more effectively to spring. A policy like this must be justified by its success; and the success can best be judged by the position of the Papacy after the Counter Reformation, at which time the Holy See stands out as an organ of the life of Europe readjusted to the new world of action and of thought. In the connecting chain between its former and its later state the pontificate of Pius II perhaps does, that of Paul II indubitably does not, appear a faulty link, although to pass from the character of Pius to that of Paul is to leave the study of the grand for that of the merely interesting. Accordingly in studying the life of Paul II, instead of speculating on the possibilities of a revived crusade, the student must unravel the intricacies of an adroit foreign policy, which ended in the complete subjection to the Pope of the patrimony of St Peter, in the establishment of the Papacy as an Italian power of note, yet one that is not too closely interwoven in the petty politics of the peninsula. He will see too the crushing of a noteworthy figure, George Podiebrad[1], King of Bohemia, who

[1] It may be said without fear of contradiction that George Podiebrad was the most remarkable man of his day. He himself would have been prepared to act as champion for Europe against the Turk, but the Utraquist heresy which divided his subjects estranged him from the rest of Christendom. His efforts to nullify this restraining condition by schemes, which extended so far as a proposal that would have modified the European state system, were bootless. He was faced by enemies within and enemies without (e.g., Mathias of Hungary) and he himself was declared an excommunicated outlaw by the Pope. In 1471 he died. In a sense the Papacy had triumphed but Mathias never made good his claim to the throne of Bohemia, Utraquism gave way to extremer forms of religious heresy and nothing had been effected towards resistance of the Turk.

had defied the Pope, and the resultant collapse of the Utraquist heresy, victories for which the see of Rome was to pay a solid price. These are the achievements not of an heroic figure but of a *cunctator*, a man who is feeling his way amid forces whose nature he cannot fathom. They called for qualities of statecraft and experience. They implied at times the taking of contemporaries into confidence; they often involved reliance upon the force of a reasoned public exposition of a point of view. For such a purpose the learned and benign castellan of St Angelo was to hand. The forty odd treatises which are known to have fallen from his pen indicate that in his case both the spirit and the flesh were willing.

It would be wrong, however, to hold that the only difficulties which faced the papal statesmen were in the sphere of action. Grave indeed were the problems which lay before them in the world of thought. The Conciliar movement, which had begun in a spirit of hopefulness and promise, had ended in general disillusionment. The ideas which had lain behind it had, to use a vulgarism, run to seed[1]. In part this may be traced to the shadow which the coming events of the Renaissance cast before them, for the Renaissance epoch proper was a time during which progress and reform were usually reached not, as is at times the case, by action deliberative and constitutional, or by subjective methods, but objectively, by vigorous executive action marked by spontaneity. It is to the credit of Pius and of Paul that they appraised at their true value the

[1] We find that the abbreviators, minor civil servants of the Papal Chancellory, irritated by the reorganisation of their body by Paul II, had the effrontery to assert in a letter of protest that they would lay their grievances before a general council. The conception of the functions of a general council implied by action such as this is illuminating.

loose talk and unsubstantial projects for the democratisation of the Church, which were put forward in this aftermath of the Conciliar period; but beyond this negative accomplishment there lay before them a constructive duty. The excesses of some of those who followed the new learning, could not obscure the fact that one of those epochs had been reached which demanded an elasticity in the Church's attitude such as the worldly wisdom of the Roman communion has displayed at many crises. In plain language it was open to Paul II to recognise, or to ignore, a tendency among those of the new learning to split into two halves, a Christian and a Pagan school. Some within the Church had of their own accord already bridged the gulf which threatened to cut them off from the new attitude of mind. Were these to be actively opposed or tacitly approved?

There was nothing unfamiliar, still less dramatic, in the points which raised the issue. Seldom indeed in history does a generation find itself face to face with an isolated issue. Thought in the Middle Ages was dominated by two principles, or favoured two directions, the logical and the mystical. Sometimes one element was dominant, sometimes the other, sometimes both were blended. It is roughly true to say that the teaching of Aristotle and Plato, grasped in some instances through the medium of single, or even double, translation, or filtered through the transforming channel of neo-Aristotelian or neo-Platonist schools, coloured, with alternating intensity, succeeding schools of thought throughout these centuries. If the Aristotelian influence, growing since the days of Abelard, culminated in the thirteenth century, the fourteenth was to see its influence challenged. There was a quickening of the Platonic influence. At first it was instinctive or romantic, remaining largely uninformed[1]. Yet in the course of time it proved introductory to a fresh interest in Plato of an unmediaeval type, both from the point of view of the moral[2] and the natural[3] scientist. In providing a learned background to the movement scholars assign supreme importance to the advent in Italy of the eighty years old Hellenist, Gemistos Plethon, who lectured at Florence in 1438 upon the works of Plato. The influence exercised by him had more than one effect[4]. In the sphere of secular philosophy his barely Christianised revival of paganism on a philosophic basis had a negative effect in its breach with Aristotelianised Scholasticism[5] and as such vitally promoted the cause of liberated thought; but also after his inspiration of pupils like the learned cardinal Bessarion[6], it became clear that a Hellenistic, a Platonised party within the Church itself was beyond a doubt in being[7]. Correct beyond a question in its opposition to the fantastic teaching of Gemistos Plethon, blind obstruction on the part of the Papacy would have resulted in the loss to the whole Church of a party which made contact

[1] Thus Petrarch kept a MS. of some of Plato's dialogues in his library on an honoured shelf though he was unable to read them.
[2] E.g., Campanella (1568-1639), Giordano Bruno (1550-1600).
[3] E.g., Paracelsus (1493-1541).
[4] F. Schultze devotes the first volume of his unfinished *Geschichte der Philosophie der Renaissance* to the philosophy of this remarkable teacher.
[5] See Georgius Trapezuntius, *Comparatio Platonis et Aristotelis*, for the impression produced by Gemistos Plethon's teaching.
[6] Creighton, *History of the Papacy*, Vol. III, p. 40, quotes a letter written by Bessarion on learning the death of Gemistos Plethon which startlingly illustrates the influence which he had had upon him.
[7] Bessarion took up the cudgels for Plato when Georgius Trapezuntius attacked the works of that philosopher with acrimony.

with an important manifestation of the spirit of the age. He would be a bold man who would maintain that under all circumstances a challenge to "the spirit of the age" is a mischievous policy for the Church and its leaders to pursue, but fundamentals were not then in question, to any large extent, and what may have been wisdom in the Tridentine Fathers might very well have been unwise in the age of Paul II.

In close touch with this scholarly, if exaggerated, revival of Platonic studies went hand in hand a revived interest in classical antiquity. Here too was nothing new as can be testified by anyone familiar with the lives of two such different men as Petrarch and Rienzi[1]. But just as Gemistos Plethon elaborated his neo-Platonic, neo-Christian cosmogony, so men turned again to recreate the glories of ancient Rome and to dabble in the construction of classical Utopias. In connection with this tendency academies were founded in various centres modelled upon that of Bessarion at Venice. They were centres of studies, rallying grounds for men of common interests. With them in general there was no reason why the Church should quarrel and, as a rule, the Church did not. The academy at Rome brought down upon itself however strong ecclesiastical displeasure, and an examination of its behaviour tends to the conclusion that in his strong handling of this body we need see no exception to the rule that Paul II in dealing with contemporary movements exercised a wise and an informed discretion[2].

[1] Those in Rome during the days when Italy was deciding to enter the European War will remember in this connection the moonlight recitations of D'Annunzio in the Pantheon.

[2] The view of the older historians that Paul II was unsympathetic to the new learning (see Bayle, *Dict. crit.*) was based upon the personal malice of Platina (*Vita Pauli II*). Creighton (Vol. III, p. 274) shows

The leading spirit of the Roman academy was a learned crank in whose veins ran the illustrious blood of the family of Sanseverini. His real name was Piero but, hating a connection which could only be acknowledged by the confession of its illegitimacy, he gladly set the fashion to his fellow academicians by the adoption of a name in the good old style, Pomponius Letus. A pupil of Lorenzo Valla, he assumed the point of view of a Rienzi, keeping clear however of any open political activities. His life, as is the case with cranks, was quite consistent. It breathed at every turn the classic spirit and carried that spirit to absurd excesses, as is the case with antiquarian revivals. To his side he gathered men of like mind, some of questioned reputation. Filippo Buonacursi, *alias* Callimachus Experiens, who at an early age found it safer to transfer his activities to Poland[1], was enrolled among his followers, while the presence of a Glaucus and an Asclepiades and a Petreius upon the roll of fellowship only emphasised, to the amusement of ordinary citizens, that members of many a Roman family had time to waste in discussions and in recitations and upon an intensive course of mutual admiration. The society was anti-clerical and even anti-Christian. It was darkly said that the brethren met of nights within the Catacombs, where their adoption of pedantic ritual and of strictly antique formularies bordered upon a parody of the early Christian church. The traces of their doings still remain and have formed the object of scholarly

---

that this biography "may serve as a conspicuous example of the revenge taken by a man of letters on one whom he had a cause for disliking." The view which I have urged presents a possible alternative.

[1] See on Callimachus' activities in Poland Zeissberg, *Die Polnische Geschichtschreibung des Mittelalters*, p. 351.

investigation. What seems certain is that a very severe attack of swollen head led them to overstep the bounds of prudence. Reforms in the Papal secretariat had thrown a number of disgruntled civil servants upon their own resources. Some of these were already academicians and from this section action seems to have developed. Threats of a pagan revival upon a larger scale were uttered. Treasonable language was repeated to the Pope passing all tolerable limits. In 1468 Paul II adopted severe measures. Orders were issued for the apprehension of Pomponius Letus, Callimachus, and the chief author of the mischief, the former Papal clerk, Platina[1]. The two former had left Rome, though Pomponius was soon handed over to the Papal officers by the Venetian Government. After a brief imprisonment, in which his conduct showed up as the reverse of philosophic or heroic, he was released and does not seem to have neglected his sharp warning. The Pope rightly discerned that Platina was the more serious offender[2]. He, like Pomponius Letus, was confined within the castle of St Angelo.

Readers of Platina's life of Paul II are given an inspiring account of the author's behaviour in adversity. According to this account, although subjected

[1] Platina, whose real name was Bartolomeo Sacchi da Piadena, had been a Papal abbreviator. Whereas Pius II had fostered the interests of the abbreviators, Paul II had cut down their number and altered their status. Platina lost his sense of proportion, wrote and uttered sedition and finally was imprisoned for four months. On his release he seems to have become a centre of mischief at the academy.

[2] See Creighton, Vol. III, p. 45 and p. 276, for the amusing correspondence between the grovelling Pomponius and his gaoler Rodericus. Paul II, although he raised no objection to the continuance of lectures by Pomponius, dissolved the academy. It was revived, however, under his successors and continued till it disappeared in the sack of Rome in 1527.

to the vilest tortures, he preserved his dignity, answered his persecutors with spirit and upheld the independence and sanctity of letters. Unfortunately we have preserved to us the actual epistles written by the prisoner. They present a wholly different picture. He wearied with his importunities not only the Pope[1] himself but anyone he conceived as able to be instrumental in obtaining his release. "I undertake," he writes, "that if I hear anything, even from the birds as they fly past, which is directed against your name and safety, I will at once inform your Holiness[2]." He defends his orthodoxy, offers his pen to celebrate the Pope's virtues and his policy, makes any and every grovelling promise if only he may be freed from prison[3]. After a year's humiliating experience Platina was liberated but not restored to favour till the election of the next Pontiff, Sixtus IV, who made him Vatican Librarian[4]. His revenge was embodied in the lives of the Popes which he then composed. The account of Paul II is distorted with so much mean and trivial gossip that it would merit no attention were it not a work of such high literary skill that for centuries it bamboozled historians of the Papacy. Creighton wisely remarks that there are few indications of Paul II's admirable qualities so striking as the triviality of what his worst enemy can find to say against him.

Severe as was the torture and the discomfort of prison life, to which Platina was subjected, it was his injured pride which gave him deepest and most lasting

[1] See Appendix A, No. 1.
[2] See Creighton, Vol. II, p. 46.
[3] See Appendix A, No. 2.
[4] For an appreciation of his great merits as a librarian see J. W. Clark, *The Care of Books*, p. 207.

pain. It must have been galling to the literary revolutionist to find his gaoler to be Rodericus Sancius, the man of all others who may be supposed to have represented in his eyes learning and literary gifts made odious by orthodoxy. It was the old story of the rebel facing the orthodox tradition; and there was no doubt this time which of the two was in a position to adopt the satiric attitude. If Platina's account can be trusted, he started his sojourn in a spirit of defiance, and his sentiments can be easily appreciated. As a matter of fact there are indications that Rodericus proved a not unkindly guardian when his charge's obduracy had once been broken down. Platina, in his later writings, never refers to him by name, a fact which is remarkable, considering the malice with which he was accustomed to pursue his enemies. It may indicate a desire to forgive, or to forget, one who in a time of personal humiliation did not press home his advantage. It can hardly be fortuitous omission.

It is Platina with whom Rodericus Sancius is associated in the dialogue under discussion, *De pace et bello*. In the introduction reference is made to the peace lately composed among the peoples of Italy by means of the Pope's benevolent interposition. This probably refers to the temporary lull in the bickerings of the peninsula which Paul II brought about in 1468. The dialogue, if this suggestion is correct, was composed during the period of Platina's incarceration. It is well to follow the words of the introduction further:

> Nothing is so effective in securing recognition for the wonder of the blessings of peace and tranquillity on earth, in our opinion, as the conviction of its supreme desirability provoked by trumpeting aloud the dignity of war and arms. It was a habit of the

ancients, on attaining a peace, to hold for the public delectation single combats among selected athletes, or other mimic battles. By analogy, in order that our delight in this cessation of hostilities may be the more abundant, we have determined upon staging a single and a weaponless contest. Thus, while we give glory to Immortal God and to his Supreme Vicar on earth, we organise a duel over war and peace, having in mind to celebrate the peace by, as it were, a kind of war. We are confident that you will find our discussion neither insipid nor uncongenial; and this will be the method of procedure which we shall adopt. With your permission I, Bartholomew Platina, will open the conflict in favour and on the side of peace, being the younger of the two and by nature a man to open argument....In opposition I, Rodericus Bishop of Calahorra, shall make every possible point against that earthly tranquillity which goes under the name of peace, alleging it to be the prop of every crime, an indefensible, selfish, unreliable and illusory condition. As regards war and military training directed to that end, I shall not only constitute myself their apologist but I shall go out of my way to sing their praises....My friend Platina will answer on behalf of peace....I shall endeavour to fix upon peace the charge of cowardice, of a lack of spirit and of sloth, while at the same time the origin, the essential dignity as well as the necessity of arms and warfare, I shall endeavour to establish by a logical process of argument that can not be refuted.

There is really much that needs explaining here. For example, how is it that we find Platina, the rebel and scoffer, engaged upon, or allowing his name to be used in connection with, a literary work which he never later mentions, and whose end is the purveying of sentiments most sober and correct? The situation precludes voluntary action on his part and substantiates the surmised date of 1468. In this year we know that he was eating humble pie. His abject attitude of mind may have extended to the acceptance of an offer of the most incongruous of literary partnerships. Speculation, need not reach so far. It is simpler to suppose that the so-called dialogue was in reality no dialogue at all, but, on the contrary, a satiric piece of composition from the pen of the kindly, if slightly malicious, castellan, pointing the moral of his charge's downfall in a treatise that really looked towards the intellectual problems of the day. There is banter in the attribution of hot youth to his supposed opponent and in the reference to warfare without weapons. These allusions would not miss their mark for the inmate of St Angelo: his readers outside would understand the satire of the whole in a way impossible at first for later generations.

Examination of the text confirms this attitude towards the dialogue. There is no striking difference in the style of the two speakers: and the language of Platina breathes, if possible, a more fervent piety than that of his opponent[1]. Finally, it is to a high degree suspicious that the author, engrossed in the development of his contentions, forgets that he promised in the preface that there should be an answer from Platina. It is not improbable that, parallel with their severe treatment of the academy, the Papal authorities considered it desirable to issue publications, which should have upon informed opinion in the papal states, and even other districts, a steadying effect. Faced on the one side by a Turkish menace, which on more than one occasion occupied the pen of Rodericus, and on the other by conduct which hampered the Papal policy at every turn, ranging from the open insubordination of Bohemia to the parochialism of almost all Italian states or principalities, the Curia might well see in the pacificism of decadence and intellectuality an inebriating poison with very wide and very bad effects. The moment was opportune for the counterblast. In giving it Rodericus once more

[1] See Appendix A, No. 3.

performed a valuable task in elucidating the Papal point of view upon these matters for those who had both learning and goodwill.

The opening argument of Platina is skilfully composed. It is sufficiently embellished with the appropriate classical allusions and arguments, while, at the same time, its main contention is expressed in language conformable to Christian standards. To pass fair judgment on his exposition of the case it is not necessary to say more than that his reasoning at times seems trite and commonplace. This is no rare judgment to pass on authors of the fifteenth century. Yet from the quaint fancies and special peculiarities that are frequently met with in their writings, save for one brief incursion into the ever popular realm of astronomical speculation, Platina's "case" is curiously free.

It starts indeed with a spirited description of the horrors caused by war, depicting the tortures of parents, wife and children disappointed of their loved one's return, he lying meanwhile without Christian burial and deprived of the rites of the Church, a corpse for vultures and wild beasts to prey on[1]. Having thus introduced the subject by a proper flight of rhetoric Platina traces the continuance of this sad state of things to the warped judgment and false standards of mankind. In forming these historians[2] are accused of being specially blameworthy in that it is their doing that the false glamour of hero-worship surrounds the so-called "men of action," who in reality are nothing more or less than murderers

[1] See Appendix A, No. 4.
[2] One is reminded of Lord Acton's sentence "After the strong man with the dagger follows the weak man with the sponge."

transferred to a public from a private arena[1]. In early, and purer, days the opinion of mankind was revolted even by the idea of capital punishment so sacred was man's body held, made as it was in the image of God[2]. Upon the enormity of interfering with God's handiwork Platina is made—surely with a touch of Spanish humour—to descant at length and in great flights of eloquence. To rob a human being of his life is to destroy the work of years of gradual fashioning. Farmers would indeed deplore the felling of a fruit tree brought at length to the stage of bearing: what must one think then of him, who would cut down the tree of life with its promise not of figs, nuts, acorns or apples, but of human activities, intelligence and qualities[3]?

Very grudgingly Platina concedes the illogical concession of most pacifists—the right of defence against aggression from without. He observes only that the spirit of aggression is contagious and that victorious defence is invariably the prelude to reprisals equally reprehensible to the actions of the party first at fault[4]. This said, he passes to constructive argument and to argument very much in the spirit of his generation.

Men, he believed, should look up at the heavens[5] and, so far as humans may, should base their conduct on the heavenly example. God, the great and good, had ended the confused state, which the Greeks called Chaos, by the introduction of a heavenly order. Of the nine spheres, between the innermost, the earth, and the outermost, on which the fixed

[1] See Appendix A, No. 5.  [2] See Appendix A, No. 6.
[3] See Appendix A, No. 7.  [4] See Appendix A, No. 8.
[5] See Appendix A, No. 9.

stars rest, there intervene seven to which the planets are attached revolving each in its own orbit. The symmetry, in which the whole is placed, is prototype of earthly concord, for this itself is nothing but the proper disposition and harmonious ordering of human beings. God too created the sun, the dispeller of darkness, Venus too, Mercury and the moon, whose ordered conduct delights God and is man's blessing. Mercury is the composer of discord. Minerva, born from the head of Jove, is Goddess alike of peace and wisdom by the aid of which former humanity obtains the latter. Her sacred emblem is the olive, green alike in summer and in winter. On His entry to Jerusalem, our Redeemer trod on olive branches (*sic*), sure sign that He brought peace not war to men. So runs Platina's argument, less convincing to present-day pacifists perhaps than to those, whose minds were nurtured in the astronomical tradition of the translucent spheres and whose tastes were tuned to the verbal quiddities of Italian literature of the fifteenth century and a technique which men were to learn in England not many decades later. Peace, Platina concludes, is natural, for who ever heard the normal person pray for war? It is divine, for to leave peace with us was the promise of the Saviour. In a passage of some real beauty he shows that the comforts of peace have physical analogies in nature[1]. He enumerates the works and arts and industries for which peace is pre-requisite. All leads to prove the hatefulness of war, the wisdom and the virtue of the Pope in ending it.

This is the case which Rodericus builds up in order that he may destroy it. His own answer is singularly uneven, both in its sufficiency for the immediate pur-

[1] See Appendix A, No. 10.

pose and in respect of the permanent interest attaching to it. Upon some points raised by Platina he is content merely to challenge the deductions from premises which he does not dispute. Thus to the argument for peace based upon the theory of cosmic harmony, he cogently points out that there is much in nature in which discord is the natural rule, and that this is true, not least of all, of man and man's affairs[1]. Even in minerals, he adds, one finds attraction and repulsion, as witnesses the magnet; while common phraseology presents the same phenomenon: one speaks of *discordant* notes, of *clashing* colours, of *different* schools of thought. Arguments like these meet Platina's points upon a level, but one may be pardoned if one does not dwell upon them. Along with verbal jugglery in derivations[2] they should be noticed only to pass on.

Nor perhaps is it necessary to follow Rodericus very closely where, misquoting and editing for his purpose passages in the seventh book of Aristotle's *Politics*, he speaks of war existing for the purpose of securing peace and thus being itself an indispensable condition. A more modern, and more telling, passage is that in which he praises war as a producer of virtues which cannot otherwise be cultivated, and as a necessary purge for a world, which would otherwise degenerate: a point of view which, if it has in very recent times spectacularly displayed to the world its essential vileness, is one, with which each European generation has had familiarity since the recording of European history[3]. "Non sine divina providentia

---

[1] See Appendix A, No. 11.   [2] See Appendix A, No. 12.
[3] The shifting tides of European thought upon the subject of the place of war in the world have not always worked towards abhorrence

bella geruntur humana in cuius potestate est ut quis bello subjuget aut subjugetur." The ring of the sentence lingers a moment in the mind, as one first reads it, not merely because the latinity is unclassical or the note struck unecclesiastical. The answering chord comes from the recollection of a very modern phrase —"Weltmacht oder Niedergang[1]." To link the arguments of the polished castellan with the philosophers of Modern Germany is to take them far too seriously. In this particular direction he is but giving the conventional Renaissance parry to Platina's conventional Renaissance thrust. It is no more, and no less, noteworthy than the massed quotation of classical parallels and precedents which figure in both the combatants' remarks[2].

Where then, it may well be asked, lies the significance for posterity of this dialogue? One may answer in the fact that Rodericus possessed the power of analysing phrases. His method was scholastic but there is something modern in the results he reached. To-day the question can be taken further, but it is

for it. John of Salisbury (1110—1182) would have blushed to use the Prussian argument of Rodericus; see the sixth book of the *Policraticus*.

[1] See *Politik, Vorlesungen von Heinrich von Treitschke*, Vol. I, p. 72 (Leipsig Ed. 1899), and compare also the theological views of Bismarck.

[2] In a few pages Platina refers to Alexander the Great, Achilles, Themistocles, Cimon, Caesar, Hannibal, Cyrus, Nero, Marius, Sylla, Pompey, Pyrrhus, Epaminondas, Philopoemen, Darius, Saguntum, Carthage, Fabius, Marcellus, the Lenaean Hydra, the Nemean Lion, Pausanias, Anthony, Camillus, Cincinnatus, Cato, Scipio major, Manilius, Ptolemy. Rodericus is slightly less profuse, as fits the argument, but from other works of his it can be seen that he was capable of just as much profusion (e.g. *Speculum humanae vitae*). His quotation of Vegetius is a case in point: "Si bella cessant ac armorum delitescit usus, nihil plebeius distat a nobili, nihil servilis a milite." This is the language of the Renaissance scholar, not the Papal civil servant.

only further on the selfsame road. The sophistries of his opponent passed under dialectical examination and the result was fresh and salutary emphasis upon considerations which the half-truths of the pacifist are often successful in obscuring. He held, as men should hold, that war, although an evil, is not the worst conceivable of evils, that, in a word, there are things worse than war. He said, and he repeated, that war must not be considered as a condition of human affairs unrelated to the reasons for which men set to wage it: that it was, on the contrary, an instrument capable of uses good and bad. He pointed out that there are nameless horrors more contaminating than recourse to arms. That facts are facts and words are words, though in superficial minds the two may be confused, he showed with cogent logic: and yet through all his reasoning the note of the idealist recurred, a warning that there was still room for the crusading spirit.

The author of the dialogue falls too into his place in the history of those who deal with Christian Ethics. That those, who take the sword, shall perish with the sword, summed up the arguments which the notoriously sceptical Platina drew from the religious sphere. The point, honestly or dishonestly held in Platina's case, is serious and needs an answer. The resources of biblical scholarship which modern theologians acquire, were not at the disposal of the bishop. He grasped, however, in rudimentary fashion that the ethical teaching of the Gospels, like that of all the world's great teachers, took as a general rule, a concrete form, and that the principles, of which such concrete teaching was but the application to specific circumstances, needed elucidation by careful thought and by the collocation of a number of such cases. Thus, in answer to Platina's point he quoted John the Baptist who, when questioned of their duty by the Roman soldiers, replied in terms at least tacitly approving their occupation, "Do violence to no man, neither accuse any falsely, and be contented with your wages." The larger synthesis which is possible to-day would explain the seeming contradiction by referring to the teaching of the Zealots in contemporary Palestine, their inadequate conception of the Messianic Kingdom, the equitable nature of the Roman rule, the hopelessness and the mischievous consequences of an armed rebellion and in particular of participation in it by the Galilean's followers. That might be one way, by modern methods, of reconciling the condemnation and the toleration of arms found side by side in Gospel teaching; and who will maintain that in method it differs from that of an age of thinkers, for whom in argument the word "distinguo" was for ever on the lips, or who will deny that there is essential similarity in the conclusions to which such method in the two cases leads? "For war in its own nature," concludes the Bishop, "is not bad; it is our fault that makes it so. Light is good, yet to invalids it may be a curse. But blame the eyes then, not the way that light is made."

There is a further point that may be emphasised in this connection. Much pacificist argument, which is otherwise cogent, errs in confusing the individual and the state. It is content with demonstrating that a certain course of conduct is obligatory upon individuals and it will take for granted that it is obligatory also on communities. It is at the least a large philosophic assumption that the state is a person in the sense that this is true of the individuals composing it. As regards the question of non-resistance, conceded that it is the duty of the individual to sacrifice himself to this extent, it cannot be assumed that any similar duty follows for the state. The moral value of the practice lies in the deliberate sacrifice of self which is required. The moral value vanishes if it is the sacrifice of others, even a minority, that is entailed, and unanimity within a state as regards such a course of action is not easily conceivable. The subject has been well treated by a recent writer[1], who points out that even were such unanimity conceivable, no one generation has the right to saddle posterity with the consequences of action so momentous for it. It is the essence of democratic government that to every generation as open a choice of action as is possible should be preserved. Now it is interesting to notice that, at least by implication, Rodericus lays stress upon the fact that matters of war and peace are first and foremost the concern of the community, and only to a much less degree of individuals. He pointed to the Roman cult of the war goddess Bellona as intentional elevation on their part of war and military virtues to the rank of national and sacred institutions not lightly waved aside. He was glad to quote, and to dwell on, the example of the Maccabees as God-inspired trustees of Israel's honour and its national existence. He traced Rome's history showing that the foundation of its greatness lay in a wisely blended policy of peace and war. He argued *more platonico* that only in a state can human beings live the perfect life, and that for the state's existence armed forces of defence were

[1] Will Spens, *Belief and Practice*, Longmans, Green & Co., 2nd edition, Lecture VIII.

necessary. He seemed indeed to rack his brains for arguments which emphasised the corporate character of military questions and duties. That public statues, raised by the community to honour famous men, depicted their subjects by preference in military dress and pose, is not for him too trivial an illustration of this point. The point matters just because the tendency of the pacifist all down the ages has been to adopt an individualistic approach in a discussion of the question.

The last third of his answer to Platina, Rodericus Sancius devotes to an analysis of peace. In great part it is a repetition of his former argument *mutatis mutandis* from the different angle of approach. Running through his whole contention is a desire to make clear and forcible the distinction between what he terms the "pax terrena" and the "pax coelestis." Modern writers have described the former by speaking of a blind or a selfish peace, one conceived or clung to in a fool's paradise. Couched in language, which varies between the syllogistic jargon of the Middle Ages and the flowery vocabulary of the Renaissance academies, it is still worth while to read this section of the dialogue in any quest in search of what men thought in different ages about war. But the main point is quickly made and retains its effectiveness to-day against those who speak of peace without discrimination into species. That is the feature of this forgotten dialogue, topical as almost all the writings of its author, aimed at current mischiefs, full of inspiration for which the immediate need has passed away. Yet one cannot handle the rare and scattered manuscripts, from which the dialogue may be deciphered, without forgetting

Bessarion, or the pin-pricks of the Rome academy, or the nettled Paul II, or the Polish question, or the other questions of the day, as one realises that in one's hand there is a key to the rich and varied contribution of a first-rate mind to one of those questions that is always in debate.

# CHAPTER II

## THE FRENCH "CIVILIANS," ROMAN LAW AND THE NEW MONARCHY

THE light which has been thrown upon that period of history in which the modern nation states took shape, has brought into full notice the part played by the revived study of the Roman Law. Writing thirty years ago[1] Mr Armstrong, for example, speaking of the rise of the new monarchy in France, said that in so far as its new-won power could be traced to any theoretical basis it rested on the authority of Roman Law, and it is common knowledge that the work of Maitland, Pollard, Figgis and others has illustrated with a variety of illuminating examples the application of this truism. If, however, it is beyond dispute that each fresh application of European scholars to the study of Roman Law was accompanied by political results of moment, it is also true that there is a danger in generalisation. The "civilians" in France, for example, were not men of one type, and their division into various schools provoked the comment of Hotman[2] in 1567. It is well then that historians should take counsel of their legal brethren, and, pending final judgment, it may be useful to record the impressions of one who has attempted to do so.

[1] *English Historical Review*, IV. 14, 1889.
[2] "En nos Universitez de maintenant il se void deux sortes et comme partialitez de Légistes: dont les uns sont hommes chaffourreurs, Bartolistes et barbares; les autres humanistes purifiez et grammairiens." *Antitribonian.*

In 1453 King Charles VII of France, by the advice of the legal reformers of his day, thought fit to ordain "que les coutumes, usages et stiles de tous les pays du royaume soient rédigés et mis en écrit, accordés par les coutumiers, practiciens et gens de chacun desdits pays du royaume[1]." Over a hundred years later Denys Godfrey (1549–1622) in editing the *Consuetudines Parisienses, Biturenses, Aurelianenses, Turonenses*, arranged them according to a classification by title, section, gloss, etc., in the order of the matters treated in the Pandects. In his glosses he was faced with not a little difficulty of definition, for words like "nobilitas" do not too easily conform to classic standards[2]. Something has certainly happened between these dates and revolutions of thought generally cause, or are caused by, corresponding changes in the world of action. Men had been introduced to the idea that for bringing order out of chaos in the matter of French and feudal usage there was much to be said for a law that was all-embracing and which knew nothing of peculiars, for a system which familiarised the nation with the notion of a *princeps*, whose will would bear with equal force on all[3]. It

[1] The ordinance of Montils-les-Jours.

[2] After dismissing definitions of "nobilitas" which do not altogether commend themselves to his judgment, Denys Godfrey professes to see the essential point in the method of its concession and quotes the definition of Bartholus:

"Nobilitas conceditur a principatum tenente. Sed plerumque expresse et plerumque tacite. Expresse autem ut per instrumenta vel vivae vocis organo, et ista dicitur nobilitas cum charta; tacite autem et in conscientia seu per indirectum conceditur nobilitas quando aliquid confertur quod nobilitatem habeat annexam ut regnum ducatus vel comitatus. Ista autem nobilitant suos posessores." See Appendix C, No. 1. *Consuetudines Turonenses*, Tit. 24, VIII, Gloss. 1.

[3] Thus Duaren writing to Sebastian Albaspinaeus in 1550 of the complicated laws and procedure then administered in France, says "...eo magis quia Romanum ius quod in manibus habemus ad amputanda

was doctrine which Louis XI or Henry IV did not find distasteful and which Louis XIV was in his time to regard as common sense.

If, however, the principles of Roman Law told for centralisation and for concentrated power, we must be careful on the other hand not to make the commentators outrun their principles and turn them into the theory-mongers of despotism by finding in their writings an analogy which, as a matter of fact, they never drew without some reservations. They were not pamphleteers even in the royal way in which Hooker might be called a pamphleteer. It is true of all of them that they were first and foremost commentators. It is interesting, perhaps significant, that in the works of Alciat, Cujas, Duaren, Doneau, Connan, Brisson and Denys Godfrey, the only royal dedications to be found are in Brisson's work on *De verborum quae ad ius pertinent significatione*, which in 1596 appeared with a dedication to King Henry III, and in the tract on duelling which Alciat dedicated to Francis I, who after all had invited him to France from Italy. The alleged retort of Cujas to those who would embroil him in religious controversy has achieved renown[1]: while in analogous circumstances

---

semel huius Hydrae capita maxime idoneum commodumque videtur." Hotman writes in favour of a code. In England too, as well as in France and Germany, the continuance of a state of legal chaos, which no jurisprudential theory of the day had power to remedy, would have ended either in personal despotism or in disaster. The French jurists were first concerned with providing an effective system for the administration of justice. For this they needed the monarchy as much as the monarchy needed them. Anything which the monarchy may have got from them in the way of a theory of monarchy flattering to monarchs was a by-product and a carefully guarded by-product. Of the slow parallel development of kingship and the common law in England the same *mutatis mutandis* may be postulated.

[1] "Nihil hoc ad edictum praetoris."

he writes expressing his reluctance to enter the arena, "cogitans quam sit alienum a studiis meis congredi cum hominibus nullo alio quam maledicendi studio praeditis[1]." The standard of reserved severity which Cujas set himself caused comment at the time, but polemics, except legally internecine polemics, were not characteristic of the French "civilians."

But there is a more important reason for using caution in attributing to the French "civilians" too rigidly monarchic views. Some opinions they express themselves will show it. There is a passage in Alciat's comments from the ancient jurisconsults on the *Digest*, book L, title 16 (*De verborum significatione*), which will provide a useful starting point.

Semper enim apud quascunque nationes ius supremum populi fuit, idque vel legis divinae institutio ostenditur. Nam cum hominem creavit Deus, illi in caetera quidem animantia ius et dominium concessit, hominum autem ut alteri alter serviret non indixit. Unde principio rerum non divina iussione, sed ex populi consensu Reges assumpti sunt: quod et post Romani imperii occasum servatum fuit, cum Carolus Magnus a populo Romano Augustus electus est et a pontifice Leone sacro oleo inunctus, quod ius populi hodie Gregoriana lege in septem Germaniae primates translatum est. Sic et Franci, Chilperico ejecto, quod regno idoneus non esset, Pipinum πανκελτικῷ consilio substituerunt. Et cum Pipini proles a majoribus degenerasset, rursus Odonem, mox eius fratrem Robertum et deinde Roberti nepotem Hugonem ad summum fastigium evexerunt: is Hugo est qui vulgo Capetus dicebatur, unde oriundi sunt qui etiamnum Francorum rebus moderantur et quod de maximis hisce regibus, nimirum Romano et Franco, dictum est, idem et in inferioribus observatum fuisse... ut merito censeam divina lege eum justum principem esse qui ex populi consensu regnet quod et Aristot. tradit: qui vero invitis dominetur, eum tyrannum esse, etiamsi Caesar sit, a Septemviris electus vel quaqua alia ratione civili iure potentiam suam tueatur.

[1] "*Pro Io. Monlucio episcopo et comiti Valentino Diensi praescriptio adversus libellum quendam nuper editum Zachariae Furnesteri subdititio nomine.*"

Unde cum magna regna non ex subditorum consensu sed per violentiam primo constituta sint merito divus Augustinus lib. de civ. Dei iiii magna latrocinia esse dixit[1]. (Ulp. lib. x. ad edict. L. xv.)

This is hardly the typical Italian utterance which caused so much hostility among French writers of that day[2]. One might almost feel that one was reading a sentence of Hotman or Postel, and that every canon of the nicest French patriotic, yet constitutional, standards had been satisfied[3].

[1] See Appendix C, No. 2.

[2] Machiavelli is one source of their discontent. But the views of this Italian School, of which Catharine de Medici was alleged to be a practising disciple, and which was accused of importing alien conceptions of monarchic government, were, as a matter of fact, being propagated in France almost from the beginning of printing in that country.

"Rex enim similitudo sive imago quidem divinitatis est in terris dum idipsum agit in limitato circumspectoque regno quod deus in universo. Hinc reges in Exodo dii vocantur. In his est provinciarum quas regunt summa potestas." This is the "fair Italian hand" of Rodericus Sancius of Arevalo, Bishop of Calahorra, a Spaniard but Castellan of the Castle of Angelo (see Chapter I). The book (*Speculum humanae vitae*) was popular. In France, Gering, Kranz and Friburger printed two editions in Paris in 1472 and 1475, when Machiavelli was 3 and 6 years old respectively, Keyser and Stoll one in Paris in 1473. Le Roy in Lyons printed editions in 1477 and 1478. Peter Metlinger one in Besançon in 1488.

[3] "Satis igitur demonstratum esse arbitramur, Regibus Franco-Galliae non immensam atque infinitam potestatem a suis civibus permissam fuisse...sed eos certis legibus et pactionibus obligatos esse." Hotman, *Franco-Gallia*, Cap. xxv. (Frankfort Ed. of 1665.)

Postel, who has grandiose schemes for the organisation of the world under the French monarchy (see Chapter III), writes nevertheless "il faut, necessairement qu'une Monarchie soit esleue et conformée au monde et prenne son fondement en la Gaule de la force et consentement du peuple Gaulois...il faut que selon mon principal penser dire et escripre, le trèschrestien Monarchie soit par consentement du peuple Gallique esleu, approuvé, soubstenu et defendu pour avoir a iamais telle authorité sur l'universel monde en choses temporelles comme Sainct Pierre jadis receut en spirituelle." (See Appendix C, No. 3.) (*Histoire des expeditions faites par les Gaulois*, pp. 5 and 95.) The popular sanction for Government is stressed both here and in the conception of the French Monarchy developed in his *La Loi salique* published in the same year 1552. See below, pp. 123, 124.

It is another aspect of sovereignty which is stressed in the following passage of Duaren taken from his comment on the *Digest*, book 1, title 4, l. 1.

Nam jus, quod princeps constituit, vim legis habet, etsi non intervenerit populi consensus sed sola principis voluntas. Sic enim accipiendum est quod hic dicitur ab Ulpiano in lib. I. Quod principi placuit legis habet vigorem: ne alias inde aliqua absurditas consequatur. Quis enim edictum Claudii pro lege habendum putet, quo admonebat populum, nihil aeque facere ad viperae morsum quam taxi arboris succum? Ut ait Suetonius in Claudio. Caesar quidem dixisse aliquando fertur homines debere pro legibus habere, quae diceret. Sed haec invidiosa oratio ac principe indigna exitium ei haud dubium attulit. Superiora verba intelligere debemus de voluntate principis ius constituere volentis, quae voluntas legis vim habet et constitutio dicitur[1].

This is the utterance of a teacher who, as the letter I have quoted indicates, believes in the simplicity of the Roman System and in maintaining simplicity within it. He believed in the danger of ultramontanism, as witnesses his *Defensio pro libertate ecclesiae Gallicanae*[2], and may thus be said in one sense to join hands with the mutually incongruous company of those whom Dr Figgis catalogued as believers in the doctrine of the Divine Right of "Kings" or civil government. That he would have expostulated against too topical or controversial an application of his views is suggested by his quotation from Seneca's epistle XIV, which he is not the only civilian of that time to quote[3]. Moreover his pupil,

[1] See Appendix C, No. 4.

[2] "Dubitandum non est quin rex qui praecipuus est fundator, tutor, custos et propugnator ecclesiarum sui regni, non solum iure possit, sed debeat dare operam et curare ut decreta et constitutiones, quibus haud dubie propulsantur ea quae diximus incommoda, diligenter et bona fide observentur." Defensio etc. § 22 (Appendix C, No. 6).

[3] "Interdum populus est quem timere debeamus; interdum si ea civitatis disciplina est, ut plurima per senatum transigantur, gratiosi in eo viri, interdum singuli quibus potestas populi et in populum data est" (Appendix C, No. 7).

Doneau, is either scholarly or antiquarian, as in his interpretation of Ulpian's famous Dictum[1], or inclined to take a frankly utilitarian attitude as to the origin of settled government.

> Ad urbes tuendas regna condita. Intellexerunt enim homines, plus esse praesidii et commoditatis ad res bene gerendas unius sapientis et regis in imperio quam in imperio aut totius populi aut plurium: quia vir sapiens vel per se vel sapientium consiliis adjutus facile ac statim consulere posset in commune, ac quae recta decrevisset, statim exsequi, cum ei omnes parerent: in plurium autem administratione propter varia hominum judicia et naturalem ad differentiendum proclivitatem facile eveniret ut distraherentur animae in diversas sententias, atque hoc modo aut tandem nihil statueretur certi; aut si quid fieret serius, interim res et bene gerendi opportunitas elaboretur[2].

In the figure of Cujas is to be found the grandest personality of the French commentators and the most massive qualities of intellect. In him detachment is a passion and not even Brisson, the legal lexicographer, is more scholarly aloof from current issues[3] than is Cujas in his comments upon the

---

[1] *De iure civili*, Lib. I, Chap IX.

[2] *De iure civili*, Lib. I, Chap. VI. See Appendix C, No. 5. This is of course Sir Robert Berkeley's argument in the Ship Money Case. "We must consider that it (Parliament) is a great body, moves slowly: sudden despatches can not be expected in it. Besides though Parliament cannot err, parliament-men may de facto: every particular member of the House hath his free voice; some of them may chance to make scruples where there is no cause; it is possible some of them may have sinister ends; these things breed delays, so they may disturbances....These matters are considerable in such cases as ours is. Wherein apparently Mora trahit periculum, and to follow the rule, Festina lente, is most dangerous." This, like Doneau's, may be an argument for royalty, but it is argument based on expediency and therefore cuts both ways.

[3] In defining the word King for instance Brisson dwells upon the Roman practice of giving that title to certain barbarian chieftains; quotes Cicero, *Pro Deiotaro*, Livy Bk. 31 anent the practice; and discusses the insignia of kingship. The manner of Brisson's death may indicate that he was of like political passions with ourselves, but in his purely legal books one would not think him such.

*Digest*, book L, title 16 (*De verborum significatione*). "Bona civitatis abusive publica dicta sunt, sola enim ea publica sunt quae populi Romani sunt." In his comment upon these words of Ulpian Cujas proceeds to an elaborate catalogue with a distinction of goods into portables, etc. His purpose is antiquarian, legal. His mind is set on undoing Tribonian, not on undoing erroneous theories as to the monarchy of France. As to monarchy he too took a lofty, but a utilitarian, view[1].

> Nam jus quod princeps facit, necessitas facit. Nam non ob aliam rem creamus principem, quam, ut decreta faciat et iura det, ut est aperte scriptum...et rectissime dicetur ab Accursio rem a populo venisse ad Senatum, et a Senatu ad principem, per partes, per vices, paulatim, pedetentimque. Quid vero inquit, per partes venit? Ut, inquit, necesse esset Reipublicae per unum consuli. Nam senatus non potuit sufficere omnibus provinciis regendis; ob id constitutus princeps, qui rerum omnium esset dominus quique potestate caeteros omnes praepolleret[2].

In the interests of that centralisation in which he conceived efficiency to lie he was ready to drive the argument home to the logical conclusion of exempting the *princeps* from the action of the laws. In his notes upon the sixth section of the first book of Justinian's *Institutes* one may read:

---

[1] It is worth noting that in commenting in 1585 (the year after the death of the Duke of Alençon made the direct right to the throne of Henry IV indisputable) upon the Decretals of Gregory IX, he writes: "Nam rex Francorum in spiritualibus alium superiorem non agnoscit quam Romanum episcopum, in temporalibus neminem, nec Romanum episcopum nec Imperatorem, quod privilegium etiam habere regem Hispaniarum scholiastes tentat in Adrianus c. 63 dist. et alii."

It is significant that he includes in this immunity from external temporal control the Republic of Venice also.

(*Recit. solemn. ad Decretalium Gregorii IX* libros 2, 3, 4. Ad cap. Per venerabilem, XIII.)

[2] *Ad tit. Digest. de Justit. et Jure ad leg.* VII. Appendix C, No. 8.

Sic, auctore Accursio, ait vires populi datas esse principi et in principem...nec vero ullo alio distat populus a principe, quam quod populus suis legibus tenetur, princeps legibus solutus est. Caeterum ut suis, ita et principis legibus populus tenetur. Principem igitur populus quem vice sua constituit et se principis legibus obligavit[1].

Here is political doctrine with a vengeance, one may be tempted to exclaim; further study however modifies the conclusion, for in his lectures on the Digest is to be found the telling disclaimer of any such intention.

Hodie principes non sunt soluti legibus, quod est certissimum, quoniam iurant in leges patrias in quas olim non iurabant[2].

François Connan, the pupil of Alciat, carries the moderation of these supposed despotism-mongers a stage further. His argument is this, taking the Lex Regia as a text on which to base it. There were, he points out, some who said that after the transference of power accomplished by this "law" the *princeps* had been left with precisely the same authority which before had been vested in the *populus*. This being so, no legislative or administrative act was within the prince's scope unless it had senatorial ratification. With this view Connan could not agree. It did not square with the dictum of Ulpian. Nor was his doubt removed by the suggestion that as *princeps senatus* the Emperor might claim to represent the senate. The transference to his mind was entire and complete. The *princeps* in no way shared his authority. The uncontrolled authority of the Emperor dated from the reign of Augustus.

[1] Appendix C, No. 9.
[2] *Ad titulos diversos Pandectarum recitationes solemnes. Ad legem* v.

Quodcunque igitur imperator, inquit Ulpianus[1], per epistolam et subscriptionem statuit, vel cognoscens decrevit vel de plano interlocutus est, vel edicto praecepit, legem esse constat. Hae sunt, quas constitutiones vulgo appellamus.

Of course no considerations of this kind could absolve the *princeps* from the binding principles of the law of nature. By these he and the citizens alike were bound by so strong an obligation that disregard upon his part might end in a duty of resistance...

ut si qui iusta haereditate rex est, tyrannicos mores induat, divina atque humana iura pervertat, suorum non salutem petat sed sanguinem, eiiciendus regno est, dum id fiat, rex est nec attentandus a quoquam est, nisi communi suorum decreto deliberatum sit et constitutum. Sanctum est enim nomen legis, sanctum et regis. Hic si tyrannus expellendus est[2].

"eiiciendus est," "communi suorum decreto," what phrases are these? It might almost be a propagandist pamphlet for the "Seize" that we have stumbled into or an excerpt from the *Franco-Gallia*. If this is to be the considered sentence of the teachers of the Civil Law, Kings might well think that they had best turn common lawyers, and the universities be checked in a course which could bring nothing with it but disaster to the royal cause[3]. In a word Connan's

---

[1] See *Digest*, I, 4. 1. 1.

[2] *Comment. Jur. Civ.* I, 8. See the following passage later in the book: "Postquam vero coepissent ii, quibus ad hunc modum fuerat data rerum omnium potestas, contra rationis praescriptionem multa pro animi libidinem facere, et periculosum videretur unius arbitrio fortunas et vitam omnium committi, quidam eiectis regibus, leges posuerunt, alii retentis regibus tanquam frenos legum iniecerunt, ut eos nimia potentia ferociantes duritia iuris cohiberent." 161. 7. Appendix C, No. 10.

[3] In England for instance Henry VIII had founded the Regius Professorships at Cambridge in 1540 and at Oxford, it is said, in 1535, though the date is more doubtful. Ten years before Francis I had persuaded Alciat to leave Milan for France where he lectured at Avignon, Bourges and Paris. Paris was not to shine as a school of law however till a much later date.

utterance went further than that of any other writer on the law here quoted.

It is doubtless the part of wisdom not to elaborate in too great detail any theory based on quotations, representative it is hoped, but all of them, to a greater or a less degree, *obiter* in their nature. This much at least is certain. The French civilians of the seventeenth century approached the study of the Roman Law from different points of view. Whether however their method of approach to it arose from a historical or from a more purely analytical predilection, whether they directed their interest more towards the content or the system, the very nature of the law they taught forced them into the position of advocacy for the centralised and universal as opposed to the decentralised and the particular. The example set by them was to be followed with profound effect by students and teachers of French Law. Dumoulin was the first only of a school which embraced names like Coquille, Loisel, Pithou and even Pothier. And who can doubt that the effect was, besides being professional, political as well. Just in so far as political partisanship was not characteristic of them, the "civilians" of the sixteenth century in France presented a united front. Their doctrine was effective because it treated of sovereignty and not sovereigns. The salutary lessons, which by inference from their writings could be learned as to the danger of impairing the unity or simplicity of the former, gained force from the remarks upon popular sovereignty to be found in Alciat, the argument from expediency to be found in Cujas or Doneau or the strong words on the duty of rebellion expressed in Connan's works. It was just this impersonality, this detachment, this reliance upon principle which was absent from other contemporary theorists. Many of these were content to see the monarchy of France, the seat of sovereignty, a prize for the more successful party in a war of wits and arms. So few had that, which alone lends nobility to the speculation of political philosophy, the conviction that institutions are instruments for a political or social purpose, not vantage points to elevate the leaders of faction, or hustings for the demagogue. The very Huguenots who after St Bartholomew applauded the *Vindiciae* or the *Franco-Gallia* were, by what one can only in charity call a change of emphasis, those who, after the death of Alençon in 1584, proclaimed most energetically the sanctity of the Salic Law. A direct sequence of events again explains the difference in the Catholic party's views in 1559 and 1588, between an adherent of the Guises during the reign of Francis II and those of the Seize, for the excesses of which the Guises were, if truth were told, responsible. For both religious parties principles seemed interchangeable, but, if the Roman jurists of the day proved no exception to the rule in their private capacity, it is not manifested in their work, and the dominance of civilisation for the third time by the Roman jurisprudence, to which end their work was instrumental, lifted the development of events out of the fashioning of religious controversy. Here join hands the "civilians" and the Politiques, the party which anticipated the modern nation state; and the new monarchy may be said to trace in part its new-won power to the writings of the Roman Lawyers, or, as these observations would indicate a better way of putting it, to the impersonal authority of Roman Law.

# CHAPTER III

## WILLIAM POSTEL, WORLD PEACE THROUGH WORLD POWER

AFTER every great European war the subject of world organisation has taken a prominent position in the minds of men. So it was in the period of the Vienna Congress, so it was, as one may read in novels of the period, after the Crimea; so it is with especial emphasis to-day. Students of the subject have been at pains to trace to its origin the idea of international law and organisation. They have pointed to this or that circumstance, to this or that individual, as the first incident, or personage, in its eventful history; and their labours have led them to excavate in distant and strange quarries. The chief point of interest however lies not so much in the possibility of tracing for the present "League of Nations" project a spiritual ancestry among say the crusaders of the eleventh, or the "civilians" of the sixteenth, century. Granted that men of different schools of thought in different centuries were moved by the international idea, the important matter still remains—to learn from the study of as many types as possible how to them, it, or kindred projects, appeared both desirable and feasible. For types of men transcend the centuries, and the grand idea, which is the object of our study, seen through the vision even of those most unusual, or those most bizarre, has been subjected to an analysis which at times may prove illuminating.

This consideration justifies a new attempt to study the life and writings of a man whose name may be generally unknown, but one whose work has occupied the attention of those interested in that "peculiar amalgam of law, ethics and theology" at the end of the Middle Ages, and at the beginning of the New World, to which international law traces its origin. William Postel was born on Lady Day, March 25th, 1510: he died in Paris September 6th, 1581. His life coincided therefore with the reigns of the French Kings Francis I, Henry II, Francis II, Charles IX and Henry III. He saw the glory and might of France under Francis I broken and dissipated during the distressful period of the civil wars. He did not live to see the wounds bound up in the reign of Henry of Navarre. It was an age prolific in great men, Rabelais, Amyot and Ronsard in the sphere of letters, de Thou and Jeannin, to quote two only among the learned statesmen, Henri Estienne, Budé, Cujas and Doneau in letters and in law, Calvin and the early Jesuits in the theological arena. In an age of controversialists he shone among the foremost ranks.

> Postel ton grand ami, qui a toute remplie
> De sa grande fureur la France et l'Italie
> Et qui a pu aussi ton esprit attiser,

are lines written to Ronsard by a poet of the times.

His Jesuit biographer attributes to him some sixty publications, many of which are rare and some no longer extant. The subjects covered are wide, philology, geography, oriental languages, astrology, history, theology: and if his learning, which in geography and oriental languages especially perhaps has remained significant, was extensive it was certainly provocative. One scholar portentously proclaims his delight in Aristotle "because there are in this divine author none of the errors of Luther, Melanchthon or Postel." Lambert Danau (b. 1530) calls him "dog" and his work a "nebulo impurissimus," Henri Estienne (1531–1598) an "execrable monster," de Serres (d. 1598) singles him out as "the father of the deists," Sutcliffe (d. 1628) deems him "an atheist," Beza thinks him "un cloaque de toutes les hérésies," while his chief enemy Mathias Francowitz (Flaccus Illyricus), in a melting mood compared to some in which he wrote, maintains that "several devils were lodged in the body of this unfortunate man: it was never he, but a legion of devils who vomitted the abominations of which his works are full." For Postel to have provoked such a reaction in a world of thought rich to overflowing with original ideas excites our curiosity. Familiarity with his life and with at least some of his less repellently obscure works shows a man noble in character, afflicted beyond the common lot and one holding views that are of interest in the sphere of international philosophy.

Postel's parents lived at Dolerie, near Barentin, in Normandy in a small and obscure fashion. They did not long survive his birth, leaving him upon the world friendless and in need. We do not know how he lived through his earliest experiences, nor how he found the chance of education. At thirteen years of age he held the post of usher in a small school at Sagy sur l'Aubette in the modern department of Seine-et-Oise. The strain of life must even at this early date have frayed his nerves and rendered his disposition crabbed, for the story runs that one of his pupils attempted suicide in deep resentment and that another stole in upon him in the night intent to kill him. He saved some money from his pay and went to Paris, where he encountered the lot of many a precocious clown and was robbed of all he owned by the first strangers he fell in with. He laboured in the fields and in time made up his losses, winning the desired goal at last, a nomination to the college of St Barbe. Here he was free to indulge in full his voracious appetite for study. He found a Jew who taught him Hebrew, he attained a more than working knowledge of Greek and, attracting the interest of a wealthy traveller from Spain, he refused his offer to return with him as secretary but did not let him go till he had perfected himself under his tuition in Portuguese and Spanish.

All through his life it seems that Postel was doomed to find a difficulty in remaining in one place. His curiosity to see a royal pageant took him to Rheims. Once there he had the offer of a private tutorship. The pupil was the younger brother of a local abbot. The arrangement seems to have been satisfactory. The boy proved apt and affectionate: Postel on his side liked the boy and many years later in 1552 dedicated to him a volume of his works. While at Rheims, or shortly afterwards, he attacked Bucer in a tract defending orthodoxy, which, however, did not win the doctorate for which it was presented to the Sorbonne as a thesis. It was never published and we have no data for judging its contents. In other lines of study his efforts won more appreciation. Though they were not published till 1538, he had been since 1532 preparing material for his first linguistic publications, the *Introduction to the Alphabets of twelve different languages* and *The Origin and antiquity of the Hebrew language and the Hebrew nationality*. The fame of his erudition reached the ears of King Francis I and his learned sister Margaret. The former was engaged on the task of adding to the royal library at Fontainebleau and he coveted in particular some oriental manuscripts. Who could be more apt for the purpose of collecting them than the youthful and acquisitive Postel? In 1536 we find him sent, with a companion Peter Giles and with four thousand crowns between them, to seek for manuscripts in oriental countries. They visited Egypt upon their journey, winding up in Constantinople, where they attached themselves to the French mission, recently accredited to the Sublime Porte under the Seigneur de Forest. The French ambassador was glad to use their knowledge of the language and the customs of the country in the commercial negotiations which he was then conducting with the Sultan. At the same time Postel made every use of his opportunities and under the tuition of a learned Jew embarked upon Chaldee and cabalistic studies.

After what seemed only too short a time he returned in 1537 to Paris, stopping at Venice on the way where he conferred upon the subject of oriental typography with the Venetian printer Daniel Bomberg. In Paris his reception was cordial and like Casaubon sixty years later, he was put upon the staff of the Royal lectors, his subjects being Greek, Hebrew and Arabic. Like Casaubon also he was destined to learn that it was one thing to be assigned a salary by a royal patron but quite another thing to receive it with regularity. The Chancellor Poyet seems to have befriended him more than once, and, outside his official emoluments, he received on one occasion 225 livres in return for special services. With the fall of Poyet from power Postel lost his lectorship. Fortunately before this happened he had been presented by Poyet's nephew, Mgr. Gabriel Bouvery, the Bishop of Angers, to a deanery, which, held *per vicarium*, gave him leisure for his occupations and, being more regularly compensated, put him outside the pressure of necessity.

If Postel's career had been terminated in his thirty-third year, in 1543, he would have been regarded as an oriental scholar of great promise and precocious achievement, whose interests extended beyond the subject of Eastern languages into the spheres of theology, geography and history. Beside the books mentioned above he had published an *Arabic Grammar* (1538), *A Description of Syria* (1540), *The Athenian Magistracy* (1541), *The Book of the Koran* (1543), *The argument of the Holy Spirit* (1543) and *The Christian Euclid* (1543). In these writings there was little to presage the coming ecclesiastical disfavour which was to be his portion, unless indeed from those nuisances which beset every ecclesiastical system, the obscurantists, to use Postel's own words, "qui hominem alicuius linguae a propria diversae peritum statim proclamant hereticum." Up to this year his ecclesiastical record was a good one. In *The argument of the Holy Spirit* he follows but in Anselm's footsteps when he proclaims his desire to establish the existence of the Deity by means of purely human arguments: while in his *Book of the Koran* he goes out of his way to attack the Protestants, dubbing them empty, or vain, evangelists. Small wonder then that his name was mentioned in connection with another palaeographical mission to the East, again with royal patronage. Unfortunately the bent of Postel's mind in these months disinclined him from the project and was destined before long to alienate official favour, ecclesiastical and royal.

Before everything Postel was a fanatic. He was fanatical in his pursuit of truth. To him the truth was personal not abstract: it was incorporated in his own experience; it became either a reproof for past behaviour, or an indication of immediate duty. The journeys which he undertook, the scenes he witnessed, the knowledge he acquired, were to him but phenomena emphasising the divine assertion that there were sheep outside the fold and the divine injunction to go forth and preach the gospel. Thus it came to pass that during the years 1540 to 1543, and with increasing intensity, Postel meditated upon, and was distressed by, the thought of the existing divisions among mankind, a standing blasphemy against the fatherhood of God.

His meditations long continued had two important consequences. In the first place he determined to devote his life to the task of healing these divisions. In the second place he sought coadjutors and found them, or thought to have found them, in the little company of seven, some of them fellow members of his College, who in a solemn mass heard together on August 15th, 1534, in the Chapel of St Denis, had laid the foundations of an association which was to develop into the Society of Jesus. In 1544 Postel went to Rome and was attached to the Society upon probation. But, if the record of the early days of the Jesuits is the record of an evangelistic enthusiasm and an international outlook not unlike Postel's, it also records the gradual development of an iron discipline which was to culminate in the ratification, by a general council of the Order in 1588, of Laynez' proposals for a despotic constitution. With institutionalism Postel was fundamentally at loggerheads; it is not surprising therefore to find that his connection with the Jesuits endured only for twelve months. Loyola publicly dismissed him in 1545 and some authorities have spoken of the subsequent relations between him and the Order as embittered. This is hardly an adequate picture of the position, for in 1553 he speaks of "consortium illud, in quo merito a nomine Jesu nomen habent, quo duce totus Oriens in maritimis est ad fidem Christi fere iam conversus," while at the end of Postel's life Paschasius says he saw him on friendly terms with members of the Order in Paris dining with them and discussing with them in the Lombardic Schools. Of his "dismissal" Postel himself writes that they indeed dismissed him, but only as St Paul "dismissed" St Mark.

The trouble lay in the method, which his mind had come to regard as the best method, for attaining the unity of mankind which he so devoutly longed to see. In 1542 he was airing his views to the Sorbonne which was unsympathetic: in 1543 he is said to have had an interview with the King himself who proved ultimately antagonistic too. His first book *The Concord of the World* was published before he left France for Italy in 1543. He was elaborating his views throughout the next ten years and in as many volumes; in essence however his contentions did not alter, and it is excusable if at this period of his life's story one is chronologically to anticipate a little and describe them.

Added to Postel's passion and his learning there was deeply embedded in his heart a tendency to mysticism. Often in expounding a straightforward thesis it seems that the very words, as he employs them, melt before his eyes into their mystical significance, and the logician becomes a dreamer. This tendency gave him his fondness for the symbolism of mathematics and made him an avid student of the Cabala. To the modern reader this disposition may well prove a stumbling-block. With Erasmus he may well exclaim "Cabbala et Thalmud, quicquid hoc est, meo animo nunquam arrisit," and it is but a step from this attitude of mind to that of discounting everything that Postel said on any subject. It is right to remember all the same that the Cabala, and cabalistic studies, worked their fascination on types of men as different for example as Pico della Mirandola, Reuchlin and the Admirable Crichton; while Bodin, the sanest thinker of his generation, in descanting upon law and political philosophy, is not out of harmony with a certain strain of thought in Roman jurisprudence—to which Professor Goudy has borne testimony—when he indulges in a to us incomprehensible excursus into the mystery of numbers. This borne in mind one can read with patience the elaborate mystical and numerical disquisitions of Postel on world concord. His obsession was the number *two*, the balanced symmetry of which he saw in all things heavenly and earthly.

Starting, as did many scholastic philosophers, he saw the double nature of universal law. There was on the one hand the eternal law, the controlling plan of the universe, existing in the mind of God. There was the natural law also or the participation of man, as a rational creature, in the eternal law, by doing which he discovers his true end in life. The nature of mankind itself was double. Beside the heart, the seat of human passions, the lower part of man, the *anima* as Postel labels it, there was the higher part, the head or brain, the *animus*, through the agency of which man alone reached the knowledge of good and evil, of what consequently was seemly in the commonwealth. For the duty, or rather the only possible action, of mankind was comprised in the interpretation and approximation of its condition to the unity of all creation which found its consummation in the simultaneous divinity and humanity of Christ. What else was meant by the petition in the Lord's Prayer, "Thy will be done, as in heaven so on earth"?

> Que doict-on entendre et demander, disant: Soit faicte la volunté en la terre comme au ciel? C'est qu'il fault du tout et en tout et partout, que toutes choses soyent restituées...à celle fin que comme nous voyons le Ciel avec ses estoilles estre resglément gouverné...par les divines intelligences, nous en semblable forme voyons après destruictz toutes les tyrannies de ce monde, tant les spirituelles comme les temporelles, et afin que la forme et imitation du ciel soit estendue sur la terre.

How could this end be brought about? The chief obstacles were the divisions of mankind. It was appalling to the mind of Postel that nothing was being done to dissipate or mollify their baleful influence. The Church did not attempt to remove even Christian differences. Writing to Maes, the Hebrew scholar and his constant correspondent, in 1563 he deplores the narrow outlook of the Tridentine delegates. For his part he was of opinion that the Council of Trent was a body more suited to confirm the Roman domination than to convert schismatics and he asks where, at this solemn gathering, were the delegates of Muscovy, Armenia, Greece, Georgia and Aethiopia. The first step on the road to the glorious end which he proposed, must be a study of the races outside Europe. It must be done with tact if it was to lead to a bridging of the gulf. His learned books about the East never lose sight of a missionary purpose. Let those who pursue this purpose in the East be all things to all men, he writes in his *Concord of the World*, before Mahommedans let them not start with asserting the divinity of Christ. At first let them emphasise in conversation the glory of God and the beauty of the world.' Later they might broach the subject of the Holy Trinity and the Messianic prophecies, and so on. For this purpose Postel knew his own suitability and to it he dedicated his strength and his learning; "aut universi animos ad Christum per linguarum variarum beneficia reducam aut in hoc negocio moriar" he writes in 1550. The idea was not original. It had been present to the minds of the fathers of the Council of Vienne when they urged the furtherance of oriental studies by the Universities. Nor was Postel alone in being struck by the idea of what could be done by Europeans who travelled through a heathen country. Grotius himself years afterwards summed up the Christian faith in rhyming couplets whereby mariners, having committed them to memory during the long hours of their watches, could, when shipwrecked, put them to good purpose by the conversion of the heathen.

Postel however laboured under no illusions as to the efficacy of such counsels of perfection. God wishing to fulfil himself in a manifestation of divine unity on earth would, Postel thought, have chosen some agent on earth through which it should be accomplished. He devoted much thought to the discovery of this agent and several books to the explanation of his conclusions to the world. He might have been expected to have seen this agent in the Papacy, or in the Church acting through General Councils, or in the Emperor. It is a fact which political philosophers will deem of interest in the record of the growing significance of the secular nation state that he found it in the kingdom and people of France. "Je suis tout assuré que le coeur et antique vertu des Francoys sera du tout resuscité moyennant la verité éternelle."

To this point he returns again and again and brings into play along with other arguments the historical. It is true that his historical argument cannot be defended by modern critics. He relies on the writings of his predecessors indiscriminately and bows slavishly to their authority, the Pentateuch, the Sibylline prophecies, the writings of Berosus, a historian who wrote in the third century a Babylonian-Chaldean history in Greek, fragments of which have been preserved by Josephus and Eusebius. His argument amounts to this. Noah had three sons; the divine curse resting upon Ham the number was reduced to two, again the mystic two! Of these Shem, the elder, inherited the levitical position, was "set apart" to become the witness to divine purpose in the world, just as Japheth, the younger, the lay brother as it were, was ordained to be the instrument of its accomplishment. Now Japheth had a son Gomer, and to Gomer as their first ancestor could be traced the history of the Gomerites, or Gauls, just as Gomer's son Ashkenaz was the founder of the Germanic races. Shem's spiritual jurisdiction descended to the Pope. The Kingdom of France inherited the duties of Shem's brother Japheth. In the performance of these duties, in fulfilling the stern purposes of God, no earthly power could be allowed to block the way, an assumption which, beside its obvious other implications, leads to the somewhat unexpected conclusion that, in all matters of this world at least, the Papal jurisdiction must yield the place to that of France.

In ruling the destinies of so sublime a nation the French Kings held a position truly awful and Postel, who was no respecter of persons, was not slow to tell them so. The King of France according to this theory became indeed God's silly vassal. "It is no more glorious to be born of exalted origin," says Postel, "than to be born with black hair." "Si autem roges," he writes upon another occasion, "uter sit potior, patricius sine laude an plebeius virtute ornatissimus, idem est ac si roges uter histrionum sit praeferendus, qui servum optime an qui regem pessime agat." It is not lost time to dwell upon this attitude because there is in Postel's writings a theory developed of an elective monarchy in France, well worth a closer study from those who trace the development of political theory throughout the centuries. For present purposes it is enough to note that in the eyes of Postel "il faut nécessaire qu'une monarchie soit esleuée et confirmée au monde et prenne son fondement en la Gaule de la force et consentiment du peuple Gauloys" and that of his life work and theories he can say "estant donc mon general but de conduyre le monde en fondement et vray principle de la concorde, union et souveraine paix par le seul possible moyen de la Monarchie Treschrestienne."

The arguments by which this theory is built up may seem strange enough to modern ears. Familiarity with the writings of the day will show them not to be exceptional. They were shared by many of his contemporaries, they were regarded by all as needing serious consideration if they were to be refuted. The phraseology is not more strange to-day than that of the pages of Sir Walter Raleigh's *History of the World* where Noah and Joshua stand side by side with oriental monarchs or with Tudor sovereigns. Moreover Postel was irrepressible: again and again he elaborates the theme. In 1548, in a treatise on the symbolism of the candelabra in the tabernacle of Moses, he presses his theory as to the divine intention of a French world monarchy. In 1551 he returns to the attack in his *Reasons for a Universal Monarchy*. The next year is given to apologetics for the French. He publishes *An account of all the expeditions undertaken since the Flood by the Gauls or French*, following it by *An Apology for Gaul* and a description twelve months later of *The Golden Age*. Nor would he rest content by exposition. In mordant terms he pillories the authors, who in their writings have done no, or insufficient, justice to the Gauls. His life was one of storm and stress but, to do him justice, he remained consistent in his views.

It is easy enough to understand however that the Society of Jesus might find one who held these views an embarrassing fellow member. It was so, partly because the Jesuits in their early days had no room for that diversity of opinion in their ranks upon the existence of which in later days Lord Acton comments; partly because in a Society predominantly Spanish and anxious to demonstrate its papalism before exalted eyes, strong Gallicanism, rather fantastically urged, produced a cleavage in the ranks. His opinions however procured him something more than expulsion from the Order. From letters written to Maes it is clear that he spent some time in prison. When and why he was thus treated, except that his arrest took place before January, 1547, and that it was in connection with his opinions, is not certain. He must have been pardoned and liberated by 1548, because in that year we find him acting as secretary for oriental languages to Pope Paul III. Moreover sometime in 1547 he paid his second visit to Venice.

This Venetian visit was to prove the second turning point in Postel's life. Events he then experienced turned Postel the orientalist and humanitarian into Postel the visionary and heretic. He had been living through a nervous and intellectual strain of no small nature. His high hopes had been disillusioned, had even ended in his personal disgrace. His opinions made converts slowly if at all. Physically he felt the wear and tear of three hard years. His poverty was abject. He experienced the scholar's need of books and, even when every penny he could scrape together was spent upon them, the supply remained inadequate. Food and vesture and even coal took a second place or were neglected altogether; "nisi admoto oris halitui calamo nil atramenti ob gelu instillari potuisset" we find him writing to a correspondent. Small wonder then that in Venice he fell ill. For some time he hovered between life and death. Returning health for his battered body had none of the tranquil indolence which convalescence brings for normal men. It was a time of fevered visions and stern self-questioning. There can be little doubt his mind henceforth became liable to aberration.

It was in the hospital of St John and St Paul in Venice that he met a woman, named Joanna, about fifty years of age, a devout woman, who tended the sick, but of whose personality and history nothing is known from any other source. It so happened that the mystical significance of the number two found for itself in Postel's mind about this time a new interpretation in the balance of the sexes. In the fantastic web which the sick man's fancy wove the good Joanna became implicated. A hundred years later, in a dirty book, indecent explanations are suggested. They may be disregarded. His contemporaries, with the exception of the insanely hostile Francowitz, never so much as hint at them and Postel had enemies enough to do so had they wished.

Man's double nature still obsessed him and it was revealed to him upon his sick bed that the year 1547 was to see final redemption or "restoration" brought within the reach of man in both his aspects. In this year the efficacy of Christ's redeeming power had been born again, acting with double, and equal, power through a double instrument. For if the old Gospel preached that man's *animus* or soul was to find redemption in Christ Jesus, it was now Postel's allotted task to demonstrate that the *anima*, the "inferior part of the spirit," needed renewal also. As man's fall was due alone to the old Eve, so his restoration should be accomplished by a new Eve. This new Eve Mother Joanna became, so he asserted, through the substance of Christ dwelling in her. Postel himself became alike her forerunner, a second John the Baptist, as also the firstfruits of Christ's redeeming power exercised mediately through her person. She it was who, by establishing his right to regeneration, opened to him through herself all the mysteries of Christianity.

Here we have, of course, another case of the religious excesses to which the Reformation and its counter movements sometimes led[1]. As a great authority upon the subject writes: "Anabaptism ranged over the whole gamut of human passions and possibilities, from the pure and pious enthusiasm of a Balthasar Hubmaier to the licentious and cruel fanaticism of a John of Leiden." Anabaptism was not alone in this; and there were not a few who speculated mischievously on the subject of Redemption, as the thirty-first of the thirty-nine articles of the Church of England indicates by the very completeness and positiveness of its assertion in refuting them. At the same time it is only just to point out that into the most blasphemous of errors, attributed to him in some quarters, Postel never fell. He never wrote, and never meant, that redemption came from the New Eve herself. To him even in his wildest moments she was but the instrument, and not the agent, of redemption[2].

If Postel's writings to this date had aroused unfavourable comment, it was as nothing to that which manifested itself when his views upon the new redemption of mankind began to circulate. He was known to have composed in 1549 his Revelations as to the Mother of the World or the New Eve, though

---

[1] And not the Reformation only—witness the career and pretensions of Joanna Southcott.

[2] The history of the Mystics furnishes more than one parallel to this instance of feminine inspiration and influence upon men of religious discipline. See for example *The Life of Blessed Henry Suso by Himself*, edited by Dr W. R. Inge (Methuen), Chapter XXXV. The record of Saint Simonism furnishes more modern analogies.

it was never printed. The growing coldness of his associates may have suggested that it was wise for him to take another journey. In 1549 he sailed from Italy for the East and arrived in Palestine the same year full of enthusiasm for missionary work among Mahommedans and Jews. His intention was to purchase manuscripts, to translate the Gospels into Hebrew, to preach in Arabic and to publish an Arabic New Testament. His plans were frustrated by his lack of means, and his funds were reduced to thirty crowns, when Gabriel de Luetz, Seigneur d'Aramont, the French Ambassador to Turkey, passed through Jerusalem on his way back to Constantinople from the Persian campaign in which he had accompanied the Sultan Soleyman. He had upon his staff some learned men, Thevet the geographer, Peter Bell, a good friend of Postel, and Peter Giles, his old travelling companion. To this staff Postel attached himself, though Giles was careful to point out, very much to his annoyance, that the royal authority to purchase manuscripts was vested in himself alone. In their company however Postel made some interesting journeys, seeing the Samaritans, the Maronites and Druses. After a visit to Constantinople of no long duration he returned to Italy in 1551. He brought back with him on this journey the famous pseudo-gospel of St James with which his name has always been associated[1]. Italian scholars and divines however made no effort to detain him so he took the road to Paris, stopping on the way at Basle and

[1] The nature of this gospel, upon which Mariolatry has sometimes been based, must have had a strong appeal to Postel with his tendency to emphasise the high position and lofty duties of women. (See *Studia Sinaitica*, No. XI.)

Dijon, at the latter place delivering some mathematical lectures. Berthot, the rector of the University, has left a record of his stay at Dijon, in which he speaks of Postel's piety, learning and discretion as well as of the University's efforts to detain him. His mind, perhaps invigorated by his travels, had shaken itself free from fantasy. If this was so the reception which awaited him in Paris was not one likely to ward off relapses. He anticipated restoration to his royal lectorship. In spite of his efforts, seconded in influential quarters, he could not attain it. In 1553 he spoke of charging for his lectures if he could not get the royal patronage. Soon after we hear of well-attended lectures in the Lombard schools, but the natural anxiety as to his future produced the recrudescence of his mental trouble. Beside works published at this time on other subjects, especially those developing his theory of the Gauls, he produced *The Book of Woman's very famous conquests*, in which is given the full fruit of his meditations on the life and death (for she had died in 1551) of the New Eve, Joanna. In a supplement attached to this, *The doctrine of the Golden Age or the evangelical reign of Jesus, King of Kings*, we read the following:

> Donc nous voyons que à la parfaicte action de nostre forme, il faut que nous ayons quatre parties, qui respondent aux quatre elementz du corps: *L'Ame* despend du corps et est constituée dedans le sang: *L'Anime* est immortel divinement crée et uni en une nature avec L'ame, comme l'element de la terre avec l'eau: *La Mente* ou la vertu superieure, ou l'intellect Agent respond au feu et se conjoinct avec L'Anime: *L'Esprit* respondant à l'air se conjoinct à L'Ame comme l'air avec la terre. Le chauld humide qui est propre de l'air est commencement de la vie en toutz animaulx et non par le chault extrême du feu elementaire...et c'est pourquoi le sexe feminin consummera la perfection du monde.

It is passages like this which can explain, if not excuse, the revulsion against Postel's lectures in official quarters. Feeling his freedom interfered with Postel left Paris at the end of the year 1553.

His departure was deliberate, for in the records of the town of Besançon there is to be found an account of the city Fathers' dealings with a, to them, unknown lecturer from Paris named Postel, who had approached them with an offer to lecture for a salary. On consulting the regents of the schools they learned more about Postel and gladly struck a bargain. The sojourn in Besançon does not seem to have been happy. A few weeks after his arrival Postel was on the road again. The termination of the appointment may, perhaps, be traced to imprudent expressions of opinion, for, a year later, a citizen suspected of unsound doctrines is at pains to prove to the authorities that he had had no sort of dealings with Postel. In Basle he stayed some months, transacting business with Operinus[1], who published a great number of his books. At the beginning of the autumn he returned to Venice.

In Venice he received a visitor of interest. The Jacobite Patriarch Ignatius had sent a representative to Europe, one Moses Meredinaeus, charged, among other matters, with bringing back printed copies of the Scriptures. Tiring of the red tape methods of the Papal officials, Moses determined to establish contact with Postel and went to Venice. He could not have come at a more opportune moment. For some years Postel had owned a Syriac manuscript and knew that the centre of Syriac studies was Vienna, where that learned Imperial Official Widmanstadt

[1] The German Herbst.

had in hand an edition of the Testament in Syriac. To him occurred the plan of sending Moses to Vienna with an introduction. It would prove, he no doubt thought, a good excuse for himself following a few weeks after with his manuscript.

All happened as he planned, thanks partly to the assistance rendered him and Moses by Cardinal Pole. He himself received a welcome passing his greatest expectations and by the end of 1553 Postel found himself installed a Regius Professor in the University of Vienna, with duties and a salary equivalent to those of his lectorship at Paris. More than this however he found a splendid patron in Widmanstadt. Mutually they inspired each other's studies. But it was not to last. After six happy months the happiness was shattered, the partnership with the learned Imperial Chancellor was broken up. With the taint of heresy upon him he left the country in great haste. We do not know the details. Perhaps his departure was the firstfruits of the recent arrival in Vienna of the three Jesuits, Canisius, Lejay and Bobadilla.

The year 1554 marks the beginning of even greater sufferings. Robbed and imprisoned under a misapprehension at the Italian frontier Postel reached Venice in a state of deep dejection. He found that he and his works had been proscribed by the ecclesiastical authorities. That some of his works might be upon the Index Postel feared, but it seemed outrageously unjust that Catholic readers should be warned off all his books. He demanded an enquiry. The tribunal after four months' deliberation passed a judgment to the effect that the author was not bad but mad. The blow was cruel, the sentence stung him to the quick. Starvation stared him in the face.

He was compelled to sell his books for 200 ducats to Otto Henry's library near Ingolstadt. One can only suppose these disasters recreated the old symptoms. A letter to Maes in 1555 speaks again of the constant promptings of Joanna and of their leaving him no peace. What final act of folly, on his part, caused the Inquisitors to act is not recorded, but act they did and the unfortunate scholar found himself in prison first at Ravenna, then at Rome, remaining there three years and six months. Once at least he attempted an escape and broke his arm in the attempt. In after years he was under the impression that Pope Paul IV meant to have had him executed. Caraffa was the founder of the Inquisition but he did not love the Jesuits. Whatever the truth concerning his intention may be he died in 1559 and in the Roman riots, which followed the Pope's death, Postel and other prisoners were freed.

The next three years were years of wandering and of disappointment. He was in Basle, in Trent, in Augsburg and in Lyons. A friend in Augsburg spoke of buying back his books from the heirs of Otto Henry, but it was never managed. In Lyons, where he published at least one book, he was again pursued for heresy, but seems to have been able to justify himself on this occasion. At last he came to Paris after nine years' absence. He boldly faced his accusers before the court of Parlement. The sentence went against him. For three months he was to be confined in the monastery of St Martin, a close prisoner; after the three months were ended it was ordered that he should remain there under supervision. In spite of this decision he was liberated and, before long, lectured to vast audiences on geography. If we may judge however from a private letter, his mental symptoms once again returned. Recent political events had made the Queen Mother anxious to avoid further brawls in Paris touching the religious, or any kindred, questions. It would appear that after kind, but firm persuasion, he resumed his sojourn at the monastery, leaving the hospitable house of Joseph Scaliger in which he had resided. And, strange to say, as voluntary prisoner, or compulsory guest, in the monastery of St Martin he found the peace which all his life he had not known. The brain cleared, the visions left him. He became the glory of the community in which he lived, for learned men flocked to its doors that they might visit the wise and ageing scholar. Nobles and senators came to hear his conversation, the learned brought him oriental manuscripts, the courtiers consulted him as to the nature and the history of the royal presents which came from Eastern countries. No inmate showed more piety or attended Mass with greater regularity. In 1564 he wrote a recantation of his errors, but, before this he was re-established in the royal favour. Catharine de Medici wished him as a tutor for her sons, but he had savoured to the full the benefits of princes and preferred his cloistered studies varied by relaxation, taken in strolling round the garden or in performance on the flute. Though with the straitest sect of theologians his theological reputation never quite recovered, he was invited to resume his academic labours. He lectured and may have rejoined the staff of royal lectors, for, in a book written in this period, he gives himself the title "Doyen des lecteurs ou professeurs du roy en la très fameuse Haccademie de Paris." On the other hand, when he stood for the mathematical professorship upon the death of Ramé, it was not he, but Bressiaeus, who was elected. In these years the fame of his learning penetrated far and wide. Francis Bacon tells, in terms a little too far fetched to be believed, of the singular virility of his old age. He died in the odour of sanctity seventy-one years old. He was buried in the chapel of the monastery.

On his tombstone was inscribed:

> POSTELLUS POSTQUAM PERAGRAVIT PLURIMA PASSUS
> PRO PIETATE POLOS PARISIIS PETIIT
> OBIIT 6 SEPTEMBRIS 1581
> MOERENS PONEBAT ADRIANUS TARTRIER MEDICUS.

In conclusion it is well to think how and why this broken life has its importance. Over it all, as over the life of Swift, hung the evil spirit of insanity. At the time when such a visitation was regarded as in the immediate and especial purpose of Almighty God, it furnished another weapon to the armoury of his theological opponents. Postel's career will not be finally appraised, "quoad ad humanum pertinet," by these, but rather by those who could see through the aberrations to the solid learning which, when circumstances allowed it, produced what they were glad to think the fruits most characteristic of his real personality. In the grudging praise of Plantin ("qui vir, etiamsi fantasticus habeatur, multa certe ingeniosa neque semper vana tractare videtur in suis operibus") through the whole circle up to the generous tribute of Bressiaeus' Inaugural Lecture ("Postelli virtutes et literas non mihi si centum linguae sint...enumerare queam...omnium est homo linguarum, omnium artium et disciplinarum, omnes virtutes (*sic*) promtuarium") there is a juster estimate and the names subscribed to it, including as they do that of Scaliger, are weightier than those of his detractors. Modern orientalists may not have paid him tribute, but learning will look with a tolerant eye on "mere Bibliography" when it chronicles the fact that, along with other notable services to the typography of oriental languages, Postel's ill-starred Vienna visit was the means of introducing the first fount of Arabic type into the German countries.

A modern historian[1] at any rate, whose life of the founder of the Jesuits gives his opinion on any learned matter weight, ranking his work on a level in importance with Mercator's, points out Postel's immeasurable superiority to preceding geographers and maintains that he was the first to give scientific geography its place in historical and theological exegesis.

For students of International Law Postel's importance is of another kind and his name will rightly be included in their works. Since men have speculated on the possibility, and the direction, of developments in international comity there has always been a school of thinkers who believe that no force but that of a single predominating power can make a system of international law an abiding influence in world affairs. According to one version of this theory the nations may agree to observe such a system by the most solemn promises or contracts, but none the less history has shown that sooner or later one of them, which has most to gain by doing so, will break away to follow, perhaps under cover of the noblest professions, interests that are peculiar to itself and selfish. There is no half-way house, according to

[1] See Gothein, *Ignatius Loyola und die Gegenreformation*, p. 373.

this school, between the perpetuation of a national system of world development and the establishment of international comity by the uprising of a preponderating power in the shape of some one nation, which will forbid the others to follow their separate divergent interests. This preponderating nation may itself be guided by self interest, but it will be argued, at an early stage in any system of society that which marks advance is the quantity, not the quality, of government. When in the settlement of international relations international law has been a force, not a mere aspiration, for two or three hundred years, then it will be time to insist that other nations beside that originally in preponderance shall have a voice in what international law shall be.

A position, worked out to this point of detail, is no doubt a modern product. It, for example, or a theory very like it, proved in the hands of German propagandists a most effective weapon in perverting the intelligence of some of the less balanced American scholars and jurists during the period of United States neutrality. This is not the place to distinguish between the truth and falsehood which lie embedded in it. Suffice to say that, after his own manner and in the language of his own generation, Postel was an early and an important exponent of this attitude of mind. As such he will figure in the text-books. The forces that controlled the world in his day, in like manner as the forces of the last five years, militated against those who would build a practice on these views. The war has emphasised what is a sound enough conception in their theory, that international law will always rest, in a last analysis, on force. It is for the nations who have accepted opposing conceptions of a law of nations, to show if they can unite among themselves and give their theories the support of force, refuting thus, by the harmony of their amalgamation, the identification of a preponderating force in international affairs with the preponderance of any single power.

# CHAPTER IV

### SULLY AND HIS GRAND DESIGN

THE "Grand Design," the famous seventeenth century scheme for world organisation, sometimes attributed to King Henry IV of France, sometimes to his minister Sully, has had, not only for political philosophers but also for practical statesmen, an appeal that does not seem to weaken as the ages pass. A hundred and fifty years or so after the death of Henry it provided Jean-Jacques Rousseau material for analytical examination: in June 1919 Lord Robert Cecil invoked its inspiration in expounding before a meeting in the Albert Hall the scheme for a League of Nations recently evolved in Paris. This last alone would make it opportune to consider over again the details, the historical importance, still more perhaps the very existence of the "Grand Design."

The undertaking justifies itself on narrower grounds. A discussion of the subject is not easily accessible in English. The *Cambridge Modern History* hardly touches on the question. Lord Acton in his published lectures condenses into one sentence of dismissal a number of passages and arguments from foreign authors still marked with his lead pencil and visible in the Acton books in the University Library at Cambridge. In France, where interest in the reign of Henry IV has reached such a pitch that previously to the war several numbers of a *Revue Henri IV* appeared under the editorship of Monsieur Albert Chamberland at Reims, a centre of French Renaissance studies, there has been written much to help the English enquirer; while in Germany, before propagandist motives in domestic or external affairs had tainted German scholarship, attention had been successfully directed also both to unravelling the diplomatic correspondence between Henry IV and the minor German potentates, as also to a critical study of Sully's *Oechonomies Royales*, the Memoirs of his years of service under Henry IV. Perhaps it will not be until a modern edition of this book is published that the material will be to hand for a final judgment on the period and on the subject.

Maximilien de Béthune, Baron, then Marquis of Rosny, Duke of Sully, was born in 1560, the year, it may be noticed, which saw the publication of the four volumes of the completed works of Ronsard. But on a shorter view 1560 was the year of an event more significant to Frenchmen, for on December 5th King Francis II died and the House of Guise fell from power. From that day forward this family, buttressed by matrimonial alliances with half the leading men of France, resting upon a natural French horror of heresy, guided by far more intelligence than has been allowed them by historians who have written under the shadow of the successful Bourbons, carried on a losing fight to regain the dominant position which they had occupied at the Court of Francis. The struggle they put up was splendid. Hardly a movement of domestic history during the next forty years can be analysed without a Guise intrigue being discovered as one of the component parts, but their hour had sounded. "When all was lost," wrote protestant Beza of the death of Francis II with good judgment, "the Lord our God aroused himself."

In the changes and chances of these forty years Sully played an honourable part and won the favour and confidence of his lifelong chieftain. At the age of twelve, being a Calvinist, he escaped with great difficulty the massacre of St Bartholomew. Subsequently attached to Henry of Navarre he took part in the future King's most adventurous expeditions, fighting by his side at Arques and Ivry, in the course of which latter battle he was severely wounded. In 1596 Sully was appointed to the Council and charged, with other counsellors, to carry out a tour through all the royal provinces to verify the accounts of the treasurers and receivers. His career as superintendent of finances began in 1599. In close touch with Henry all the time, financial and political administration was blended with policy in that happy degree which makes demands of fortune, and of which the Cromer-Kitchener *régime* in Egypt, during Lord Salisbury's last period in office, furnishes a perfect modern specimen. In 1609, when Henry wished to embark upon long meditated projects, the finances of the kingdom had been refurbished, the military machine had been brought to a state of high efficiency, a state debt of a hundred million francs had been met, the revenue raised from nine to sixteen millions, and a reserve of twenty-two millions had been piled up.

Of Sully himself it is not difficult to paint a picture. He lived in a time of men of forceful, often eccentrically forceful, character and amid events which sharpened character, not polished it to sameness. No one more consistently than he could boast a life of service for "the religion," yet his conviction as little withdrew him from the world, like Calvin, to build an holy city, as, though he had played no meagre military part, it thrust him into the hurly-burly of contemporary life like many of those rugged warriors from Gascony, cavaliers of Huguenotism, almost any one of whom might have deserved the strange, but noble, epitaph made for one of their number fallen on the field of battle, *homme digne des guerres civiles*. Adequately read in the philosophy of history and in particular of military history, as his memoirs show him, his counsel lacked that intellectual quality which enabled Jeannin to give Mayenne the right advice when the Seize cast a bolshevist pall over the life of Paris at the end of 1590: a quality which, though Sully had had his share of diplomatic missions, caused Jeannin to be selected in preference by Henry IV to hold a "watching brief" for France in the Low Countries, when those exhausted states were negotiating for a peace with Spain in 1607. Sully was vain, long-winded, not over scrupulous and jealous; yet these characteristics were set off by abilities which contributed in a preponderating degree to that vast stock of unique qualities in his public servants, upon which Henry IV drew with such wise selection that he left the greatness of France laid on secure foundations and bequeathed a policy which, had that very greatness of France not intoxicated his successors, might well have averted the suffering that France, and the world through France, has since then been forced to undergo.

Neither his personality nor his conduct in handling the public monies, nor his implacability in pursuing his private feuds, were likely to keep Sully immune from attack, or to mollify the attacks when made upon him. His memoirs are full of passages in which he refuses to share with anyone the credit for success; while even more than the always debatable questions arising from the incidence of taxation, the method of collecting or allocating revenue, his habit of life and the standard of state he kept, which were seigneurial and very gorgeous, laid him open to a growing volume of criticism which was not long before it hardened into hatred. Against all attacks arising from such animosity Henry IV stood as a sure shield but Sully's authority did not long survive his master's death. He retired to his estates, particularly residing in his château at Villebon. From this retirement, which was broken, it is true, by half-a-dozen visits to the Court, of more importance than has always been realised, he was destined to see the machinery which he had created grow rusty from disuse and the policy, in the striking out of which he had played the chief part, give way to a chaotic situation which the advisers of the boy monarch seemed powerless to end. Nor, when the strong arm of Richelieu dealt faithfully with anarchy and chaos mongers, can it be said that this elder statesman's position was the happier. True he was created Marshal of France by Richelieu but only to make vacant his post of Master of the Ordnance. Elder statesmen, who find their positions insufficiently realised by king and country, tend to drop into reflections and reminiscences. Not in the rural surroundings of a Machiavelli or a Bismarck did Sully compose his *Oechonomies Royales*. The story of its composition forms one of the oddest phenomena in the history of authorship.

This age is not likely to be unfamiliar with the idea of the domestic splendour of public men whose life of service to the community has been no less profitable than it has been successful. The dining hall and its equipment at Villebon were magnificent: the chapel was not less stately because the devotions held in it were simple. Eighty lacqueys had been known to be upon the sick-list at one time, writes Sully's private physician, and their absence not to be so much as noticed. At any rate they hang round by dozens in attendance, when the duke or his wife left the raised terraces of the château grounds to wander of a summer afternoon through the lower gardens among the statuary and fountains. Years of devotion to King Henry had not wrought this in Sully that he had the king's easiness of access and that spontaneity of transacting business, of which one often finds shocked mention in the despatches of the Venetian, or the Spanish, diplomatic agents at his court. It was not to be expected therefore that the act of autobiography would be either lightly undertaken, or would be carried out without due ceremonial regard for the solemnity of the occasion.

When the manifold activity of the day's administration was at an end, the landowner and the magistrate were laid aside and Sully retired within the closed doors of his library. There, seated upon a chair of state, secretaries read to him those portions of his life which they had prepared that day after a careful sorting of his papers and an elaborate comparison of the records in his strong room. Day by day the manuscript grew but the publication of it was delayed. In 1638 the first instalment, in two volumes, appeared from his private press at the château, to be followed very shortly by a second edition. The very publication was attended by fresh clouds of mysterious, or rather intentionally mystifying pomposity. The printer was indeed sent for from

Angers to Villebon but the volumes open with the assertion in the course of an elaborate address to "the wise and judicious readers" that they were printed at Amsterdam by "Alethinosgraphe de Clearetimalee & Graphexecon de Pistariste imprimeurs" in that city. The second part consisting of the third and fourth volumes were published twenty-one years after Sully's death in 1662 at Paris under the supervision of Le Laboureur.

It is difficult without prolonged quotation to explain to how great an extent a work, written in the second person, is the despair of modern readers. The form in which it was cast made niceties of composition difficult, though it was a form convenient for covering up the author's traces and for throwing dust in the eyes of his readers. Mr Tilley bears witness to two sentences, one of six hundred, the other of nine hundred words in length. Apart from this however he must be an intrepid reader whose faculty of apprehension does not boggle at summaries of Sully's virtues in the fawning elaboration of an eternal vocative; while as a specimen of the process reduced to an absurdity taken from the more private passages of Sully's life, Sainte-Beuve very aptly quotes the following:

> De ce pas vous en allastes voir Mademoiselle de Courtenay, envers laquelle vous et vos gentils hommes fistes si bien valoir ce que c'estoit passé, que cette belle et sage fille vous fait en affection, et peu apres vous l'espousastes: l'amour et gentilesse de laquelle vous retint toute l'année 1584 en vostre nouveau mesnage, ou vous commençastes à tesmoigner, comme vous avez desja bien fait auparavant en toute vostre vie, en la conduite de vostre maison, une oeconomie, un ordre et un mesnage merveilleux.

Fortunately however the secretaries were compelled at times to use the direct letters, notes or memoranda of their master, while Sully himself occasionally deigned to introduce what he himself calls "un petit conte pour rire au mileu de tant de choses sérieuses." Some of these, which can be picked out of the bulky volumes of Michaud and Poujoulat's edition, are worth reading, dealing as they do with simple anecdotes of Sully's life well told; a humorous encounter at an inn, with de Bois-rosé, who nursed a grievance against him, de Bois-rosé speaking his mind freely on the subject of "un seigneur qu'on nomme de Rosny," unaware of whom he was addressing[1]: or the ludicrous conversation between M. de Roquelaure and the Archbishop of Rouen, the illegitimate brother of the King, who had some scruples about marrying the King's sister, Catharine, who was a protestant, to the Duke of Bar[2]. These and several of King Henry's letters relieve the task of reading through the memoirs, but the best commentary on their strong and weak points is the fact that in 1745 the Abbé de L'Écluse des Loges rewrote the whole of the *Oechonomies Royales*, making a smoothly running story of it, all in the first person. This made a pleasant book, which was most inaccurately translated into English in 1756 by one Charlotte Lennox, a pensioner of the Duke of Newcastle, but it must be read under a comprehension of its limitations.

It is in the *Oechonomies Royales* that the historian is introduced to the conception of the "Grand Design," that system of world organisation which Sully attributes to Henry IV and about which controversy has revolved among historians. It will be well to see how it is represented in Sully's pages.

[1] Michaud et Poujoulat, Vol. XVI, p. 145. This edition of the *Oechonomies Royales* is quoted throughout.
[2] Michaud et Poujoulat, Vol. XVI, p. 306.

Here it is that the investigator of the "Grand Design" is faced with the first of his difficulties. The papers, letters and records of diplomatic transactions scattered about in the *Oechonomies Royales* introduce the idea of the "Grand Design" again and again but in such a manner as can only provoke confusion. Sometimes it is treated as a serious matter of negotiation between Henry IV and the other potentates of Europe, Elizabeth, the Landgrave of Hesse or the Prince of Orange. Sometimes it is treated merely as the subject of King Henry's day dreams. Sometimes it becomes a useful handle in negotiations between Henry and his recalcitrant protestant subjects, like Lesdiguières or the Duke of Bouillon. All sequence in narration and consistency is lacking. Confronted with this difficulty the adroit editor in the reign of Louis XIV, L'Écluse, gives an account embracing as it were the chief features of the plan at its high water mark. Modern historians have often been content to take this account at its face value, and round this picture of it public opinion has tended to crystallise. It will serve here as a point to start from.

"Le roi," writes the pseudo-Sully, "voulait rendre la France éternellement heureux: et comme elle ne peut gouter cette parfaite félicité, qu'en un sens toute l'Europe ne la partage avec elle, c'était le bien de toute la chrétienté qu'il voulait faire, et d'une manière si solide, que rien à l'avenir ne fut capable d'en ébranler les fondemens."

The means suggested by the King to bring about so blessed a result could at first only provoke scepticism in the mind of Sully: "par la même raison, ce qui m'arrêta le plus long temps, la situation générale des affaires en Europe, et des nôtres en particulier, paraissant de tout point contraire à l'execution." More mature reflection however convinced him that many of the difficulties could be removed if a persistent policy directed towards that end was followed in finance as well as in internal and external matters. This persistent policy could only be effective, if it were unsuspected, a fact which accounted for the silence of the King to all—save Sully—in the matter.

The basis of the policy was conceived to consist in the reduction of European balance of power to an equilibrium. This, it was thought, could be obtained by a grouping, or a regrouping, of the Powers into six hereditary monarchies, France, Spain, England, Denmark, Sweden, and Lombardy: five elective monarchies, those of the Imperial possessions, the Papacy, Poland, Hungary and Bohemia: four republics, the Venetian, the Italian, the Swiss and what he terms the Belgic. These fifteen Powers should form a General Council consisting of sixty-six persons, chosen from all proportionately. These sixty-six, rechosen every third year, should assemble as a Senate to deliberate on any affairs affecting each or all, discuss their joint or several interests, pacify their mutual quarrels and determine any civil, political and religious questions touching European nations, whether as regards themselves or as regards their European neighbours.

This council might be fixed in its location or ambulatory; divided into three grand committees, according to geographical convenience, or undivided and indivisible. Its constitution should be easily changed so as to give it adaptability to circumstance. Two general considerations only should, or might, be written into the charter of its foundation: first, an obligation upon all to combine counsel and forces, if it were necessary, against the Turk; second, the application, by all the members of the Federation, of those rules of religious tolerance with regard to Catholics, Lutherans and Calvinists, which were coming into force in France.

The simplicity of the scheme, as described by L'Écluse, will be deceptive to the reader. However simple in itself, in the pages of the *Oechonomies Royales*, the story of its conception is obscure, and there is a lack of consistency in the account of the various steps by which its consummation is alleged to have been pursued. One may quote, as an instance of Sully's obscurity in telling how or when the project was first conceived, the description[1] of a famous interview given him by the King on February 15th, 1593, in which he is consulted as to the desirability of Henry making "some accommodation" with his opponents in the matter of his religious beliefs. Sully was not altogether opposed to such a step but poured out, to already convinced ears, a passionate request for the continuance of religious toleration for the Huguenots. Among the other arguments which he urged, or alleges that he urged, on that occasion, was the impossibility in any other way of prosecuting Henry's "high and magnificent designs for the establishment of an universal most Christian republic... composed of all those Kings and potentates who profess the name of Christ." This would undoubtedly be a very pertinent consideration and one proper for the Minister to urge on such an occasion, but it is mystifying to find that, to judge from another passage in the book, three years later the King seems to have

[1] Vol. XVI, p. 110*b*.

forgotten that he ever cherished such a project or, at least, that he had ever spoken of it to Sully in a manner which would justify such strong words on Sully's lips in 1593. In 1596 one sunny morning[1] in the garden terrace of the Château Gaillon, Henry, warmed by good news from the Province, expanded and, while waiting for the hunt to start, enthusiastically unfolded to Sully the "ten desires" as he named them "of his heart."

> "The ninth, my friend," says Henry, "is the ability to carry out before I die, two specific magnificent designs which I have in my mind, without ever having communicated them to anyone, about which...I shall not say anything to you now, never perhaps to anyone, till I see that by the general establishment of peace throughout my Kingdom, I have the means for the complete execution of them."

Was Henry thinking of the "Grand Design"? If not, why had it so faded from his mind since earlier days, as not to be classed among the ten desires of his heart? If it was the "Grand Design," how could he have forgotten Sully's knowledge of it from those early days, a point upon which all Sully's utterances lay such stress? We must find reconciliation in inconceivable forgetfulness upon the part of Henry, or we have in other parts of Sully's narrative to be on our guard against habits of inaccuracy, of which this forms a specimen.

Old men however as they grow garrulous will grow forgetful. It would be pedantic to make too much of inconsistencies like these. Unfortunately Henry's preparation for the actual execution of the "Grand Design," as told by Sully, presents not less but greater inconsistencies than his witness to its origin.

[1] Vol. XVI, p. 242.

Before passing final judgment it will be well to see how Sully would have us believe that it came about.

According to a passage in the first part of the *Oechonomies Royales*[1] in 1601 when the King was visiting Calais and Queen Elizabeth happened to be at Dover, the King received a letter from the Queen speaking with vexation of their inability to meet, because of certain matters of consequence, about which mutual consultation was desirable, but concerning which she dare not put anything on paper. Puzzled by the phrase the King decided that Sully should make a voyage to England, as if upon a private errand, leaving it to the Queen's pleasure to use his coming as a method of communication. Everything turned out as Henry planned. At Dover Sully encountered, as by accident, Cobham, Raleigh, Devonshire and Pembroke. He had hardly settled into his apartments before he was summoned to the Queen. At several interviews the whole circle of the diplomatic problems of the day was covered by discussion.

When Sully returned to France he maintains that an agreement had been put on paper between the French and English monarchs, which however he is careful to point out never reached the stage of signature. In effect this agreement provided for

1. A loyal and perpetual association, a fraternity, and a community, of arms and plans in the contemporary European diplomatic situation.

2. A common understanding in matters of religious policy.

3. An agreement upon a joint attempt to invite into such a fraternity, and upon identical terms, the northern, i.e. the Scandinavian, Powers.

[1] Vol. XVI, p. 364.

4. Agreement to approach the north German principalities as to methods for strengthening themselves by federation, as to enlisting their joint or separate cooperation with the present scheme, and as to reasserting the freedom of the Imperial election.

5. Agreement as to the joint duty of assisting the Netherlands in their struggle with the Hapsburgs.

This, so far as it is possible to gather, is the account, which Sully would have his readers believe, of the results of his English visit, although the visit is twice described by him[1] and the differences in detail are not easily reconciled. How far the agreement, thus evolved, might have received subsequent confirmation by the parties concerned in it, or, what is more important for our purpose, how far such political understandings, if they ever existed, would have later been caught up into something in the nature of a "Grand Design," is a matter of idle speculation for, as Sully points out, in the year 1603 Elizabeth died and with the coming of her Scotch successor the diplomatic approaches would have had to be made anew.

According to Sully the first news of the death of Queen Elizabeth reached him in a letter written by King Henry himself and dated Nancy, 10 April, 1603[2]. The letter expresses great distress on the King's part at losing so good an ally, so cordial an enemy of the Hapsburgs, one with whom he was on the verge of concerting great designs, "as none knows better than yourself having been employed in them." The hopes of obtaining such cooperation from her successor were not good. Sully must make up his mind to undertake a journey to the English Court

[1] See also Vol. XVII, p. 327 *b*.  [2] Vol. XVI, p. 426.

to sound the mind of James I and to turn the situation to the best purpose possible.

Thus it was according to Sully that he paid his famous visit to London of which any history of England bears record. He sailed, armed with all kinds of greetings for the royal family and with instructions, in part official, in part confidential[1]. The official instructions largely enjoined upon Sully the duty of congratulation and enquiry, of sounding English royal and ministerial opinion as to the situation in the Netherlands, as to a double marriage between the English and French royal children, commercial agreements and the freedom of the seas. The secret instructions contained more concrete proposals, which Sully might or might not find useful, with reference to a joint policy of hostility towards the Hapsburgs. In neither is there any mention of the "Grand Design," nor is any phrase used from which the contemplation of that project can be inferred, except perhaps a clause providing for the equal distribution among all the powers of any territories taken from the Imperial family: the inference being that no one power should by the accretion of such territories upset the equilibrium of Europe. As however in this passage we find mention of the *King* of Sweden, and as Duke Charles did not assume the title of King of Sweden till 1604, which assumption was not recognised by other Powers till 1606, doubts are thrown upon the contemporary character of the provision.

Arrived in London Sully was handsomely received. His stay there was protracted. He had many interviews with King James upon whose impressionable

[1] Vol. XVI, p. 432 onwards.

mind he appears to have worked with much success. It was not alone the diplomatic dexterity of his visitor which drew King James away from the more cautious counsels of his chief advisers. The same year a priest, named Gwynn, had been arrested on a voyage to England, and had confessed, with an alacrity which threw doubts upon his sanity, that he was bound for London to murder King James, his consort and his ministers. The ground was well prepared accordingly for Sully's whispering of dark designs on the part of Spain, of Austria, the Jesuits and His Holiness.

Six years afterwards in a memorandum printed in the *Oechonomies Royales* Sully sums up the result of this mission to the English Court[1]. The main result was a definite, though secret, agreement, signed at Hampton Court, by which James promised to allow the levy of soldiers in England and Scotland for the defence of Ostend. It was agreed that the French King should pay the expenses of this force, although a third part of the cost was to be deducted from the French debt to Great Britain. Beyond this progress had proved difficult towards a mutual understanding in the sphere of foreign politics, particularly in the building up of that re-arrangement of the European powers which, according to Sully, occupied so firm a position in the French King's aspirations. True he asserts that he had discussed these matters with James, and with some of the representatives of other European Powers in London, and had won some acceptance for his views, an acceptance the importance of which, to judge from other passages in the *Oechonomies Royales*[2], gradually swelled in his mind till

[1] Vol. XVII, p. 329.   [2] E.g. Vol. XVI, p. 491 *b*; Vol. XVII, p. 220.

he could be found writing of it as a definite agreement. All the same, on his return he had to run the gauntlet of criticism by his colleagues for lack of concrete achievement on the English mission while he himself speaks[1] of the "froideur, lenteur et timidité" which characterised the temperaments of those foreign statesmen who at this solemn moment had contented themselves with expressions of general approbation concerning not very definite schemes for a geographical reorganisation of Europe, a general toleration for the three religions, freedom of trade on land and sea, compulsory international arbitration and such self-denying ordinances on the part of all the powers as customarily accompany schemes for world organisation. The general impression that Sully desires to give is that, after his mission to the court of James, the King, perceiving a lack of whole-hearted co-operation on the part of England, turned from 1603 onwards towards the lands across the Rhine to win from the German princes support for his designs.

So much for Sully's account of the King's efforts, between say 1593 and 1603, to build up a "Grand Design" by diplomatic methods. Before examining his account it will be well to recapitulate the salient features. According to this account the idea of forming a "universal most Christian republic" occurred to Henry IV some time before he won a secure position as the King of France. Mingled as such an idea must be with an anti-Hapsburg policy, notions somewhat similiar very naturally occurred about the same time to the Queen of England. Henry having been approached by her, Sully was

[1] Vol. XVII, p. 320.

sent on a mission, which was preserved, then and since, as the profoundest of State secrets. With England however a shadowy agreement was sketched out, some of the component parts of which were suitable to form the nucleus of the "Grand Design." To this agreement the assent of other nations was to be gradually and discreetly wooed. The death of Queen Elizabeth came as a shock to Henry, who, on the very day he heard of it, wrote to Sully suggesting that he should at once fare to England to see if, peradventure, anything could be saved from the wreckage of the vast Anglo-French projects. Armed with instructions, from which such confidential questions were naturally enough omitted, Sully paid a prolonged visit to England. There, after negotiation with King James and with the representatives at London of other foreign courts, he concluded a practical agreement on the urgent question of the defence of Ostend but, though he received a sympathetic hearing, the more confidential object of his mission had to be postponed to a more favourable moment.

This is an accurate account of the project of the "Grand Design" reduced to the baldest statements and drawn from the confused and contradictory narrative of the *Oechonomies Royales*. Modern research, and a very moderately attentive reading of that work, throws upon even the broadest features of it the very gravest doubt. Of the negotiations with Elizabeth it may be said that her letter to the King, suggesting a conference on mysterious matters, is probably a forgery: indeed Sully himself[1] in later passages attributes to Henry the initiative in the

[1] Vol. XVII, p. 327.

matter. It is of much greater significance of course that, up to the present, no reference to Sully's visit has been found in any English or French State papers or in private documents. It seems almost inconceivable that there should be no reference to it in say the Hatfield papers. None such has yet been published. The suspicion under which the visit rests grows to certainty when, not only is it realised that Queen Elizabeth was not in Dover at that time, but that Sully's account of the visit contains other chronological impossibilities.

Of Sully's later English visit his narrative, as was shown above, begins with a letter to him from the King, speaking of the news of Queen Elizabeth's death. It is dated Nancy, April 10th. From Fresne's edition of the *Lettres missives* it will be observed that on April 11th the King was still without the news. As a matter of fact he heard it on the way to Fontainebleau, after leaving Nancy. The letter is therefore at least doubtful. Its genuineness is not confirmed by the suspiciously admirable way in which it both introduces the "later" mission of Sully and at the same time hints that his dealings with Elizabeth in 1601 render him the right man for the purpose. While finally—to take no further example of Sully's contradictory and confusing treatment of the "Grand Design"—how is it to be explained that in another passage we find him writing[1] as if it was only in 1607, and in that year for the first time, that the project had seemed feasible?

Neantmoins voyant que, de temps en temps pendant cette dernière année 1607, et quelquefois assez fréquemment, vostre Majesté renouvelloit telles propositions, me commandant depuis

[1] Vol. XVII, p. 213.

peu plus expressément qu'elle n'avoit point encore fait, de mediter avec plus d'attention sur icelles...dont est advenu qu'en examinant toutes circonstances et toutes humeurs et conditions...il m'a une fois semblé avoir trouvé des moyens et des fondemens par lesquels plusieurs inconveniens, accidens et difficultez qui m'avoient auparavant effrayé, se pourroient surmonter ou grandement alleger.

Well may a painstaking though not highly inspired German critic of the *Oechonomies Royales*, reflecting perhaps over the labour spent on many a preceding passage, almost pathetically exclaim "Von allen Verhandlungen, von allen Bedenken, die vor jene Zeit fallen, sagt er sich los[1]!" The whole story of the "Grand Design" is traceable to one book: after critical examination of that book any literary jury would pronounce a verdict of not proven.

Nor is it only from the printed edition of the book that doubts arise. In the Bibliothèque Nationale there exists the original manuscript from which the book was printed[2]. It appears that the manuscript was finished in its final form, though many versions were probably drawn up before the final form was reached, in or about the year 1617. That manuscript twenty-five years ago was collated with the printed text by a distinguished scholar[3]. Important differences between the two immediately appear. In the written version there is no mention of the visit to Queen Elizabeth; nor is there throughout the manuscript any use of the words "république très chrétienne," the phrase invariably employed in the printed version by Sully in connection with the "Grand Design." Moreover though some of the letters from

[1] See Ritter, *Abhandl. d. k. bayer. Akad. d. Wiss.* III, Cl. XI, Bd. III, Abt. Munich 1871.
[2] Fonds français 10305, 10307, 10308, 10309, 10311, 10313.
[3] See Charles Pfister, *Revue Historique*, 1894.

London exist in the manuscript, all those are missing which in the printed text purport to give an account of Sully's more confidential conversations with King James or with the other statesmen whose opinion he sought to sound upon his project for world organisation. Often too letters from or to Sully will differ considerably in the printed form from the written version; and in almost every case the fact, and in many cases the actual form, of alteration goes to build up a theory of later and tendencious manipulation on the part of the author or his assistant secretaries. These alterations made between the years 1617, when the manuscript was finished, and 1638, when the *editio princeps* was published, are the work of Sully's last twenty years of life, the fruit of his musings in retirement and of his perception that the destinies of France had passed from his hands for ever. In these added and interpolated passages, made when the reign of Henry IV had already become history, one finds the elaborated construction of the "Grand Design," its amphictyonic council of the fifteen Powers, its senate, its arbitral powers and the suggested regulations for procedure.

In these features of the "Grand Design" there is nothing to surprise the historian of the period, though modern popular opinion has either hailed them as a novelty or argued from the originality of their nature an anachronism indicative of later forgery. The truth is that there is nothing original about them. The sixteenth century in France, the century of Bodin, saw a development of political philosophy and philosophic speculation concerning national and international government which has been to some extent overshadowed by the work of the French eighteenth century philosophers, and so forgotten. Beside Bodin's great book we have those provoked by the Massacre of St Bartholomew, such as the *Vindiciae contra Tyrannos* of Duplessis Mornay or Languet and the *Franco-Gallia* of Hotman. But there were others in these stirring times less well known, forgotten till some historian of European thought stumbles across them in the neglected corner of a library: the work of men, who once had a European reputation, like the crazy orientalist, William Postel[1], expelled from the Society of Jesus for the grandiose nature of his French patriotism, or the benevolent Catholic priest of Paris, Emerich Crucé[2]. Huguenot writers too seemed to find a special pleasure in elaborating schemes of government in meticulous detail, Jean de Ferrières, La Noue and others; so much so that one writer has seen in certain passages in the history of d'Aubigné an instance of close collaboration with the author of the *Oechonomies Royales*. The provenance of Sully's notions one can hardly hope to trace, but that they were startlingly original it is impossible to argue in view of the following extract from *Le Nouveau Cynée* published by Crucé in 1623.

Neantmoins pour en préuenir les inconveniens (the impossibility of making at any one moment an enduring peace) il seroit necessaire de choisir une ville, ou tous les Souverains eussent perpetuellement leurs ambassadeurs, afin que les differens qui pourroient survenir fussent videz par le jugement de toute l'assemblie. Les ambassadeurs de ceux qui seroient interessez exposeroient la les plaintes de leur maistres et les autres deputez en iugeroient sans passion. Et pour authorises d'aventage le jugement on prendroit advis des grands Republiques qui auroient aussi en ce mesme endroit leurs agens....Et qui seroit le Prince si temeraire qui osast desdire la compagnie de tous les Monarques du Monde? Les villes de Grece se rapportoient a l'arrest des Amphictyons....

[1] See Chapter III.   [2] See Chapter V.

Ceste Compagnie donc iugeroit les debats qui survindroient tant pour la presence (questions of precedence from which Crucé feared trouble) que pour autre chose, maintiendroit les uns et les autres en bonne intelligence, iroit au devant des mescontentements, et les appaiseroit par la voye de douceur, si faire se pouvait, ou en cas de necessité par la force.

The "Grand Design" then, as Rousseau discussed it, as Voltaire laughed at it, as Lord Robert Cecil quoted it, was not the conception, or ideal, of King Henry but the creation on paper of his wisest minister. Is the forged evidence merely testimony to the insatiable *amour propre* of Sully? To answer this in the affirmative is to take a shallow view of history, which does far short of justice to a man, who, though he showed himself capable of forging evidence for the low end of fastening infamy upon the individuals he hated, was none the less whole-heartedly a lover of France and of the monarch, who for him typified all wisdom and all kingly skill. Nor need it be supposed that the ideals, which Sully chose to advocate in his last years were only the creation of a disappointed statesman. They may well in his mind, though not on paper, nor elaborated to their final form, have preceded his retirement. The guiding principle of French foreign policy had been antagonism to the Hapsburgs. A wave of anti-Spanish feeling had made it possible for the throne to be secured for the house of Bourbon; *La Satire Ménippée* showed no less anti-Spanish feeling than the contemporary literature of England. One understands Henry's success the better not so much by the study of State papers as in the reading of a play like Beaumont and Fletcher's comedy *Philaster*. Hatred of Spain moved Burleigh and King Henry to watch each other across the English Channel in earnest anxiety to detect the first sign of weakening in what both regarded as a common cause. On the death of Elizabeth, despite the treaty of Vervins, Sully's first duty was to incite in her successor an apprehension of the machinations of the Hapsburgs. Towards a struggle with that house all the statecraft, financial or political, of the government of France was aimed. The vast forces of men and money and munitions, accumulated by Sully's skill when the affair of Cleves-Jülich disturbed the peace of Europe, can only be accounted for by supposing that Henry felt that the struggle between him and his great European rival was now imminent. Sully saw all this but he saw also beyond and round it. He visualised, as few of his contemporaries, the greatness of the struggle. It was with him an urgent matter that France should not stand alone. In fighting the Austrians and Spaniards he wished to have upon his side the great northern German Powers at least and, if possible, Great Britain and the Scandinavian Powers. Nothing could be more helpful in the struggle than to have across the Rhine a number of allies, to whom France might tender its protection but whose activities it need not fear. By convincing such states of the disinterested aims of France, there would be at its very gates a northern, for the most part protestant, Germany at ease but impotent to pursue a hostile foreign policy. Thus it behoved French statesmen to form a league in Germany and to persuade into that league all the primary and secondary powers in and out of Germany. Towards that league France must adopt an attitude of selfless benevolence. The spoils of war must not be the object of French cupidity; France must bear rather more than her share of war's sacrifice and perils. The diplomatic correspondence between Henry on the one hand and the Landgrave of Hesse or Christian of Anhalt on the other shows with what great success Sully had impressed these views upon his master. True it was not without a struggle. "Hé, quoi," the latter is represented as exclaiming on one occasion, "voudrez vous que je dependisse quarante millions pour conquestre des terres pour autres sans en retenir pour moi. Ce n'est pas là mon intention, mon amyi." But he did convince the King and the policy bore fruit in the great anti-Hapsburg League concluded at Halle in 1610 between the German princes[1].

Then came the assassination of King Henry. From his château in retirement Sully must have watched during the next twenty years the negation of every principle of caution, or of preparation before action, upon which the policy of the preceding reign was built. Is it to be wondered that at last he lifted up his voice and spoke, using the most striking form of utterance within his power to drive home his admonitions and to sound a note of warning? His royal master, like King Arthur, should come again to earth, linked with certain arresting ideas in contemporary thought, and provoke the little men of the succeeding generation to salutary thought such as might still save the State. He is not unique in falsifying history for a purpose. The bulky volumes of the memoirs of his contemporaries lie open for proof that in this he was not singular, Lesdiguières, Epernon, Nevers and Bassompierre, all, save Duplessis Mornay of whom this cannot be alleged. To a method of fanciful conceits and of high lights and shadows, which cannot be estimated accurately apart from the literary custom

[1] See Baudrillart's article in *Revue des questions historiques*, 1885

of the French Renaissance, which too is a feature at this period of its prose as well as of its poetry, even of its historical writings and its scholarship, he added the greater freedom which was given him by devolution of authorship to his four secretaries, so that his very pomposity is seen not to be without an element of calculation. Tested in this fashion his writings resume their place as historical authorities of the first importance and the personality of Sully is rescued from the vanishing process to which it was subjected by some critics of a recent generation. This borne in mind and bearing in mind too the political forces with which he strove to wrestle, perhaps to no book more than to the *Oechonomies Royales* can be applied, at least in a special sense, the much discussed dictum of a Cambridge scholar—history is past politics and politics contemporary history.

# CHAPTER V

## "THE GRAND DESIGN" OF EMERICH CRUCÉ

In predicting the future of the League of Nations as I have already indicated statesmen and writers have been led to draw analogies from the past and to consider it in its historic aspect. There has been more than one reference, for instance, to the "Grand Design" dreamed of three hundred years ago by Queen Elizabeth and Henry of Navarre. Historical research has shown, if the contentions of the last chapter are justified, that the "Grand Design" was not conceived by Henry and that Elizabeth had never heard of it. The instinct, however, to seek in France of the sixteenth century for the grammar and the primer of international organisation is defensible. In the scores of books, treatises, tracts and pamphlets published in this period, on the nature and the origin of government, there is no tendency shown to bound conceptions of government with the nation state. It does not detract from Grotius, the father of International Law, who lived when the flames of this unparalleled intellectual activity were beginning to burn low, to say that he provided juridical expression for the conception of a family of nations which other men than he had already opposed to the cold and individualistic nationalism of Machiavelli. It was his genius to employ in this direction the strong sense of reality and power of analysis with which he was endowed. So doing he was able to build upon rock. Others had his vision without his sense and their work has passed away.

Of French thinkers in the sixteenth century none stands out as a more daring speculator in the realm of international relations than Emerich Crucé. It is not astonishing that his name has been forgotten—had even to be recovered by the researches of historians—for the book upon which his claim to fame is based had almost vanished from the earth. His modern editor, Mr Balch of Philadelphia[1], knew only of three copies. Yet in its day it quickly achieved a second edition, its author was well known and sister volumes from his pen—in particular his edition of the works of Statius—form the basis of an academic wrangle which attracted considerable attention, among its critics being Gronovius, the friend of Grotius, who attacked it very violently.

We know that Crucé was born in Paris about 1590 and that he died in 1648. He was certainly born a Frenchman, was a Catholic and possibly a priest. Evidence drawn from his works would indicate that he was widely read in the authors of classical antiquity and the "civilians." Nothing else is known for certain, and we must leave the author and discuss the book.

The first edition bears the following title-page:

> Le Nouveau Cynée ou Discours d'Estat représentant les occasions et moyens d'establir une paix generalle, et la liberté du commerce par toute le monde. Aux Monarques et Princes souverains de ce Temps. Em. Cr. Par. A Paris, chez Jacques Villery, au Palais, sur le peron royal. MDCXXIII. Avec Privilège du Roy.

[1] I have used Mr Balch's translation throughout, but have taken the liberty of occasionally altering a word to one more commonly used in Cis-Atlantic circles.

## "THE GRAND DESIGN" OF EMERICH CRUCÉ

How steeped the writers of that day were in the tradition of the classics is apparent enough in writings meant for the ordinary man's enjoyment, witness the plays of our English Marlowe, Shakespeare, Fletcher or Ben Jonson. The publicists too thought their writings none the worse for a classical allusion. Hence Crucé takes his title from Cyneas the Thessalian orator and sage, whose wisdom so impressed King Pyrrhus that that monarch attached him to his court and entrusted him with diplomatic missions and business of State, much in the same way as a modern President of the United States linked to his machinery of government the services of a wise, though silent, man from Texas, Colonel House. The treatise hung upon this title is not lengthy but covers a great stretch of ground. The object around which it centres is the attaining and the preserving of perpetual peace.

Very wisely the author places as the first object of consideration the duty of each monarch to see that internal peace, quiet and prosperity is made sure of for his state. He directs the attention of his imaginary princely reader in turn to considerations concerning commerce, currency, canalisation, the extirpation of pirates, the furtherance of education on sound lines, and the policy that should be adopted by the state towards religion. Each of these points is treated with a large amount of detail, and on each he has some shrewd remarks to make. Nor is he merely repeating the catchwords of the date. Free-trade and protection were words which meant much in these days, and had done since Charles IX had imported from Italy one René des Biragues, garde des Sceaux in 1571 and Chancelier of France in

1578, the founder in France of a school that followed a high doctrine of protection. Crucé held wider views, following in this the almost free-trade principles of Bodin, principles which however that writer proceeded to modify by very numerous exceptions in favour of limited protection.

"It is reasonable," writes Crucé, "that the Prince levies a few honest pennies on the merchandise which is brought in and taken out of his territory: but he must in so doing use moderation as much as he possibly can, and especially about merchandise necessary to life."

There is here an embodiment of the theory of excise rather than of protection. Other passages in the book confirm the theory that the conceptions that lie behind the latter philosophy of trade did not appeal as much to him as to most of his contemporaries.

His projects for the construction of canals and the making navigable of rivers are certainly not lacking in boldness; nor are they informed by any narrow spirit of patriotism.

"One finds," he writes, "enough fine rivers in France, but they serve only to drown the fields and the neighbouring inheritances, as was demonstrated to the council of King Charles the ninth, who had resolved to look into the matter if the troubles which subsequently arose had not broken up this plan....Money and trouble would be well spent in that, but it would be more useful for general traffic to join two seas....The last plan to join the seas was more successfully carried out by Charlemagne. For he coupled the rivers Altmühl and Rednitz in Franconia, one of which falls into the Danube, and from there into the Mediterranean: the other joins itself to the Main and the Rhine and falls finally into the Ocean of Holland...but while they were at this work, the rains were so great that they filled the ditch with mud. It would be easy to finish this design if there were peace in Germany."

The two seas were joined in time, but they had to wait two hundred and fifty years, and then the necessary work was not undertaken by a French King but by the most relentless of French enemies, after a peace disastrous to France and sown with the seed of future European wars; but it is interesting to find foreshadowed by Crucé a development of German canalisation, which within thirty years of the Peace of Frankfort was to give Germany, and Prussia in particular, 8750 miles of canals, of which 5041 were main streams, 885 composed of channelled rivers and the rest canals proper dug in the fashion which Crucé had projected.

The views of Crucé upon piracy do not call for particular attention save to say that he was in favour of a combined effort on the part of all the European powers for suppression, and that the pirates when taken should be settled on the land and made to work, thereby winning for themselves a permanent habitation and centre of interest, which would withdraw them, and retain them willingly withdrawn, from their nefarious ways. This method, which Crucé is careful to point out, was put into practice by Pompey in his dealing with the pirates of his day, seems also to accord with the best principles of modern reformatory philanthropy! His devices for catching the pirates before reforming them take their place in the history of savage warfare and of naval history, but need not be dwelt on here.

In his scheme of education Crucé assigns the first place to medicine and mathematics, a practical view which accords with his little concealed preference for practical men.

> Now what brings commodities to a monarchy is not the multitude of priests, ministers, nor monks, although I think their dignity is great and necessary to attract the favour of Heaven.

Neither is it the practitioners and officers of justice, who should not be in such great numbers as they are in some places. In short there is no occupation to compare in utility with that of a merchant....

After such an expression of opinion one is not astonished to learn that

one cannot recommend the study of mathematics and medicine too much, if one consider the breadth of their subject, and the grandeur of their practice beside the certainty of their demonstration....Theology surpasses our capacity. Dialectics is only subservient and an aid to other sciences. Physics is a knowledge of nature that depends on experience. Rhetoric is superfluous. Jurisprudence is not necessary and a good natural judgment is sufficient to finish law-suits....Grammar, poetry and history are more specious than profitable.

Here is something of the spirit of Cobbett's famous utterance that he would rather see people eat bacon than read Bacon.

If Crucé was a priest he was a latitudinarian. Perhaps this is scarcely the right description, for speaking of Luther and Calvin he exclaims,

What a mess they have made with their tongues and writings under pretence of reforming the abuses of Christianity. Such men must be anticipated, and forbidden to dogmatize in public or in private under penalty of rigorous punishment.

Still he understands the position of the latitudinarian, the "religion of all sensible men," as a cynic called it, and is prepared to meet it in a practical spirit by emphasising for such men the importance of good conduct as a guide in life. It was indeed this motive which prompted him to write his book.

We see an infinity of men who do not consider themselves obliged to believe except what reason shews them, whereby indeed they recognize a God, but cannot consent to other articles of the creed....Such men conform outwardly to the belief and custom of their country for fear of being described as atheists; which in truth they are not, and it would be more in point to call them incredulous, since they only follow reason and spurn theological faith as if it were only an imaginary virtue. The number of such people augments every day. For this reason the most renowned preachers concentrate on the recommendation, in their exhortations, of the moral virtues....

At any rate he will take up no other attitude less consistent with the broad humanity of every nation.

Who am I a Frenchman to wish harm to an Englishman, a Spaniard or a Hindoo? I cannot wish it when I consider that they are men like me, that I am subject like them to error and to sin.

But Crucé has no bitterness, like some latitudinarians, in maintaining his opinions, and he proceeds to demonstrate the futility of religious persecution with a sweet reasonableness that could have provoked not the most hardened defender of the faith. Indeed throughout his writings he preserves his sense of humour and there are touches from time to time delightful in their quaintness. Of the religious policy of Henry IV of France, he observes that that monarch was the first to discover that it was easier to maintain two religions in peace than to preserve one by war. Preaching probity to Emperors, he holds up the example of Alexander Severus, "who hated thieves so much that he could not even look at them without feeling sick"; while Basil the Macedonian was so anxious to do justice that finding a clean charge sheet one day in a court of justice he sent a runner through the streets to enquire if there was no one who felt himself aggrieved, and finding no one "cried for joy and rendered thanks to God."

Such were the predilections with which Emerich Crucé approached the problem of world organisation for the sake of securing perpetual peace. The world in which he lived was weary of war, gradually becoming convinced of a stalemate in France, so far as the rivalry of the various extremists was concerned, and finally experienced in the results of the appeal of such extremists to outside succour, whether in the direction of Spain or in the direction of the Protestant Reiters of Germany.

> O que c'est grand erreur, que c'est grande misère,
> De vouloir s'aïder aux Guerres d'aujourd'huy
> De bras de l'Estranger, et des Armes d'autruy
> Incognues à nous, qui sont ou trop gesnantes
> Ou trop larges pour nous, ou pour nous trop pesantes.
> . . . . . . . .
> Maudite guerre, hélas! n'estoit-ce assez que France
> Eust souffert paravant si grand perte et despense,
> Si tu ne venois or la ranger par dix ans,
> Donner aux estrangeurs les biens deus aux enfans?

Thus movingly writes Jean de la Taille in 1562. To set state against state, to profit by the evils that afflicted neighbouring peoples seemed to Crucé not only wrong but foolish policy. A lack of settled government in a country might on the one hand create a profitable vacuum, but disorder also was infectious.

> "It seems to me," he writes, "that when you see the house of your neighbour burning or falling, that you have cause for fear... since human society is one body of which all the members are in sympathy in such a manner that it is impossible for the sickness of the one not to be communicated to the other."

It would appear from this that he would have understood the Bolshevistic menace to the world at the present moment, and the international aspect of the advantages of settled government.

# 'THE GRAND DESIGN" OF EMERICH CRUCÉ

Tyranny is unfortunate, I confess, but popular fury and confusion is still more to be feared. [In the republics of Ancient History] the citizens were always quarrelling. Then followed massacre, pillaging and confusion, so that the greatest tyranny in the world would not have caused half these evils for which their best remedy lay in the domination of a single man.

The problem must be, however, when once all symptoms of internal combustion were allayed, to prevent monarchs and governments to "take their exercise" in disputing with their neighbours.

Opinions are changeable, and the actions of men of the present time do not bind their successors. To prevent the inconvenience of this it would be necessary to choose a city where all sovereigns should have perpetually their ambassadors, in order that the differences that might arise should be settled by the judgment of the whole assembly. The ambassadors of those who would be interested would plead there the grievances of their masters and the other deputies would judge them without prejudice. And to give more authority to the judgment, one would take advice of the big republics, who would have likewise their agents in the same place. I say great Republics, like those of the Venetians and the Swiss, and not those small Lordships that cannot maintain themselves and depend upon the protection of another. That if anyone rebelled against the decree of so notable a company, he would receive the disgrace of all other Princes, who would find means to bring him to reason. Now the most commodious place for such an assembly is Venice because it is practically neutral and indifferent to all Princes; added thereto that it is near the most important monarchies of the earth, of those of the Pope, the two Emperors, and the King of Spain. It is not far distant from France, Tartary, Muscovy, Poland, England and Denmark. As for Persia, China, Ethiopia and the East and West Indies, they are lands far distant, but navigation remedies that inconvenience, and for such a good object, a man must not refuse a long journey.

These remarkable sentences in which the core of his proposal is contained, is followed by a long dissertation upon the precedence to be observed by the representatives in conclave. From disputes about this Crucé seems to have dreaded serious trouble. He suggests, however, trying to speak from a purely impartial point of view, that the Pope should come first, followed by the Emperor of the Turks ("especially as he also holds the city of Constantinople which is the twin equal of Rome; also it bears the name"), next the Christian Emperor, next "as a Frenchman" he hopes he may be allowed to place the King of France, then that of Spain. "The sixth place can be contested between the Kings of Persia, China, Prester John, the Precop of Tartary and the Grand Duke of Muscovy." The kings of Great Britain, Poland, Denmark, Sweden, Japan, Morocco, the Great Mogul and other monarchs from India and Africa come next, "all brave princes who maintain themselves and do not depend on anyone." Any potentate displeased with this order will do well to lay his case before the assembly. Such is Crucé's solution of a problem to which he evidently attached importance. It is a short matter to retail it, but in the original the treatment is immense, all history is ransacked for argument, the Bible, Justinian, French provincial customs, Bodin's writings, all subjected to a close analysis with a view to finding evidence that bears upon the point.

Of more interest to the modern reader are his views as to the machinery in motion.

> The cities of Greece submitted to the decree of the Amphictyons, and those who did not obey them, encountered resentment not only of the country but also of strangers: as Philip of Macedon demonstrated to the Phocians, and took occasion to wage a cruel war against them, because they had been condemned by the Amphictyons. And the ancient princes of Gaul, although they had their lordships and sovereignty apart, handed over their differences to the advice of Druids, upon penalty of being excommunicated

and abominated by the whole people. Nevertheless never was a council so august, nor assembly so honourable as that of which we speak, which would be composed of ambassadors of all the monarchs and sovereign republics *who will be trustees and hostages of public peace*. And the better to authorize it, all the said Princes will swear to hold as inviolable law whatever would be ordained by the majority of votes in the said assembly, and to pursue with arms those who would wish to oppose it. This company therefore would judge then the disputes which would arise not only about precedence, but about other things, *would maintain the ones and the others in good understanding; would meet discontents half-way* and would appease them by gentle means, if it could be done, or, in case of necessity, by force.

There is a singularly modern note about the phrases in italics, recalling alike the mandatory theory of the recent Paris scheme and the idea, so often emphasised by the supporters of that scheme, that the Secretariat-General is not a mere machine of registration but is also charged with the functions of a watchman, a sentry, a vedette, as well as a pro-bouleutic body acting for the larger conference; that, in other words, a way out of international problems is to be found only in an organisation working with continuous activity rather than with spasmodic efforts. Is it too far fetched to put alongside the utterance of Crucé that of a famous pamphlet composed by General Smuts?

It is not enough for the League to be a sort of Deus ex machina, called in on very grave emergencies when the spectre of war appears; if it is to last it must be much more. It must become part and parcel of the common international life of states, it must be an ever invisible, living, working organ of the polity of civilisation. It must function (*sic*) so strongly in the ordinary peaceful intercourse of states that it becomes irresistible in their disputes; its peace activity must be the foundation and guarantee of its war power.

Mankind's idea of the nature of the corporation has grown richer and more varied in the three hundred years that have passed since the publication of *Le Nouveau Cynée*, and it does not go for nothing that General Smuts is a trained lawyer of the Cambridge school, but all the same the germ of the theory which the General's pamphlet presses was familiar to Crucé. He had a firm grasp of the principle that it must not merely be the function of a League of Nations to adjudicate upon disputes, but rather to foresee and dissipate the causes of hostility.

In other ways as well the author shows that his project was not a mere spontaneous expression of vague aspirations. He had a grasp of fundamental difficulties such as can be gained only by hard thinking. One of the first considerations to be faced in treating of world government is the fact that the geographical phenomena with which one has to deal, are in a state of flux, not fixed. It is not merely, as Lord Robert Cecil has pointed out, that it is dangerous to attempt to fix for ever by cast-iron treaties the limits of each nation, a contingency avoided in the Paris scheme by providing that when change is necessary it shall be after discussion and debate rather than by means of war or violence. More subtle than this, however, is the apprehension that every man must feel lest the very suggestion of the necessity for a League of Nations has not always proceeded throughout history from parties interested; that if Henry IV had formed the project of a Grand Design it would have been in reality an anti-Hapsburg measure of French foreign policy; that British statesmen to-day are concerned in general form to preserve the *status quo*. This of course would not necessarily be harmful in itself or disastrous to the world, if the power and position of the interested party were eternal. Yet empires rise and fall, and as it is the turn of each to start its way along the road of Nineveh and Tyre perpetual agreements are provocative of strife, objects of jealous resentment to the powers whose vigour is not so impaired, instruments of contention rather than sedatives. Modern statesmen in facing this difficulty to-day trust in part to the educative influence of the "New Order" upon all the nations, and in particular upon the people of those nations, partly to the extension of the membership of the League to its widest limits, including therein a repentant Germany, Austria, Turkey and Bulgaria of which they have satisfied themselves of the existence. The width of the membership proposed by Crucé for his league was remarkable at a time when for most men the *raison d'être* for its existence would have been, as was the case of Sully for example, co-operative European action against the Turk. At the same time he approaches the difficulty from a different point of view and harnesses it to drive his contention further home.

We do not know yet all the countries of the habitable earth. There is perhaps some people towards the Occident or South.... Nothing can save an empire, except a general peace, of which the principal means consists in the limitation of the monarchies, so that each Prince remains within the limits of the lands which he possesses at present, and that he does not pass beyond them for any pretences. And if he finds himself offended by such a restriction, let him consider that the limit of the kingdoms and lordships are set by the hand of God, who takes them away and transfers them when and where it seems good to Him...if he has some things to complain of, let him address himself to this great assembly, as to the most competent judge that can be imagined. This is the principal way of establishing universal peace and upon which all others depend. It is in this way that a beginning can be made. For so long as sovereigns remain separated...they will try to aggrandise themselves. But if they are content with their present fortunes, if they hand over to the people their claims as they should do, if they unite with the body of this assembly, of which they are members, there is nothing that can retard a good peace or break it.

This use of the argument that, to use Crucé's words in another place, "God is not constrained to continue his benediction in one place" is after all, on a last analysis, the only answer to the dilemma presented by the truism that geography is a dynamic not a static science.

These are the main conceptions presented by *Le Nouveau Cynée*, a work worthy of more general study; for the political philosopher he has interesting reflections on the nature of sovereignty and the effect upon it of participation in a world *régime*; for the economist he has some sound remarks on currency which in the opinion of his learned editor allow him to be classed with Nicholas Oresme, Copernicus and Gresham; for the historian there are presented problems as to the connection between his views and the insertions made by Sully in his memoirs late in life upon which the "Grand Design" is based. But Crucé has a more general appeal. A campaign has been inaugurated for the education of the country upon the recent League of Nations scheme. Ideas have been revived that have long been dormant. The man in the street will be challenged to think in unaccustomed ways. At such a time it is healthy to realise that there are few ideas likely to be promulgated that men did not think about and write about three hundred years ago. Emerich Crucé treated some of these ideas and in a vivid and arresting style. As a great French scholar, learned above most men in the history of thought, once wrote, "Il est bon de s'apercevoir qu'on a des aïeux."

# APPENDIX A

## PASSAGES QUOTED IN CHAPTER I

1. Here is one extract from a letter to Paul II: "Excussit nobis lacrymas, Beatissime Pater, adventus tuus ad sanctum Petrum, excussit gemitus, quod beatitudinem tuam comitari et applausu prosequi, quemadmodum solebamus, non licuerit. O nos miseros, O nos infelices quibus tuo suavissimo ac sanctissimo conspectu frui non licuit," etc., etc., in the same unctuous strain. Vairani, *Cremonensium monumenta*, p. 31.

2. Sed unum tibi, Beatissime Pater, de me atque his polliceor; Deum et sanctos super hac re testes facio, si nos libertati reddideris, si tua sanctissima ac liberalissima manu paupertatem nostram aliquantulum levaveris (nolumus magnas divitias, paucis contenti sumus), habiturum te fidelissimos servos (Pomponius Letus and himself) et indefessos tuarum laudum praecones. Celebrabimus et prosa et carmine Pauli nomen et auream hanc aetatem quam tuus felicissimus pontificatus efficit. Vairani, *Cremonensium monumenta*, p. 30.

3. In a passionate appeal for the abolition of warfare he exclaims: "Parcite sanguini vestro: ex eodem parente geniti sumus; ad easdem sedes, si boni, erimus" which are words attributable to Platina only after he had undergone an almost inconceivable amount of chastening! "Ego vero, ut de me ipso loquar, Virg. illud non sine horrore et exanimatione lego:—

> Haec finis Priami fatorum, hic exitus illum
> Sorte tulit Troiam incensam et prolapsa videntem
> Pergama, tot quondam populis terrisque superbum
> Regnatorem Asiae. iacet ingens litore truncus,
> Avulsumque umeris caput et sine nomine corpus."
>
> (*Aen.* II, 554).

has a speciousness which is suspicious.

4. O miseros, o infortunatos parentes, o derelictas et destitutas conjuges, o genitore expectato orbatos filios! Quid quod majorum sepulchris et solo patrio carentes, sine honore, sine pompa funeris, nullis exequiis, nullis justis persolutis, tamquam brutorum cadavera insepulti jacent, alitibus et feris expositi....etc., etc.

5. Factum est scriptorum culpa, maxime vero historicorum, qui, quo plures quis in proelio interfecerit, eum triumphos, statuas, trophea, honores tum divinos, tum humanos merito assecutum ostendunt....Quae stultitia quaeso ista est, eum, qui unum hominem occiderit, nefarium et scelestum putare; et eum qui centena millia perdiderit...colere ac divinis honoribus prosequi.

6. Moti hanc ob rem majores illi, qui novae generationi propinquiores fuere, quasi mentis divinae magis participes, delinquentes exilio mulctabant, eisdemque aqua atque igni interdicebatur, grave nefas putantes quamvis malos, tamen homines et Dei similitudinem prae se ferentes supplicio capitis afficere.

7. Quod si rustici satam arborem et prope adultam, ut jam fructus inde sperari possint, excisam dolent et queruntur, quanto magis lamentanda mors illius est, a quo non baccae, non nuces, non acini, non poma, ut ab arbore, sed auxilium et consilium et necessarii vitae humanae fructus expectantur.

8. Sed quis est, qui potentiam adeptus, illam teneat, quam justitia ac virtutes omnes commendant? Facilius enim exuberans flumen ob potentiam aquarum inter ripas continebitur quam exultans et insolens victoria hostis.

9. Utinam tandem humanum genus oculos, pulsa erroris et ignorantiae caligine, ad coelum tollat! Intelliget profecto, se ad id natum esse, ut quoad fieri possit, Deum Optimum Maximum imitetur, qui fugata illa vetere omnium rerum confusione, quam Graeci vocant Chaos, mundum hunc, cujus pulchritudinem et convenientiam ob aeternam pacem admiramur, creavit et composuit. Novem enim Orbibus, vel potius globis hunc, quem una appellatione Mundum vocamus, sapientissime distinxit. Summo illi circulo, qui omnes continet et cui perpetuo inhaerent stellae subjiciuntur septem quos errones Latini, Graeci planetas vocant. Hi contrario motu acti natura feruntur. Illam conficiunt harmoniam, qua nulla profecto major in terris audiri potest. Hanc coelestium corporum pacem non immerito dicamus; cum pax nihil aliud sit, quam convenientia et quasi conjunctio hominum inter se.

10. Sed quid ego haec exempla divina atque humana commemoro cum elementa inanimata quidem, unde haec nostra corpuscula originem trahunt, pacem expetere videantur. Agitatum ventis mare, quam terribile sit visu, quam perniciosum accolis et nautis, norunt, qui currentium undarum, tamquam ex manu

conserta, ictus et procellas cum naufragio nonnunquam perpetiuntur. Idemvero, cessante vento, quiescentibus undis, quam pacatum, quam portuosum, quam navigantibus utile, ut etiam nolentes mercatores sua tranquillitate attrahere ad se et allicere videtur. Vagantes tum pisces, pace ubique parta, littus et altum pro libidine petunt, nec allidi in saxa aut rejici ad littus, quod undis fieri solet, verentur. Amplius pascuntur in littore aves, nidificant tuto halcyones, quibus non alibi, quam in maritimis locis ova parere et incubare licet. Idem etiam nobis et animantibus omnibus ex aere contingit...moerent aves, ingemiscunt animantia, ut ait Hesiodus, et latebras, vitandi mali causa, quaeritant. At ubi serenum effulsit et pax est reddita terris...gerriunt tum aves, gestiunt quadrupedes, ac reliqua animantia et quasi securitatem macti, sese ad id, quo natura feruntur, effundunt, praeteritorum malorum parum recordantia: tanta est praesentis boni voluptas.

11. Nulli rei creatae quies data. Una species aliam exagitat, leo lupum, lupus canem, canis leporem insequitur....Nosti ut in animalibus Aristoteles voluit, basilicum reliquos sibilo terrere et fugare et vicu perimere...volucres nunquam non vides bellantes. Galli enim sese calcaribus impetunt, adeo ut mirandum sit, tantum invidiae et superbiae in tam parvo esse animali. Anseres vero, cum armis careant, clamoribus et alis sese exagitant, ac rostris verberant.

Ut tandem ad homines veniamus; quis non cernit inter conjuges repugnantias, querelas, suspiciones, in ipsos filios indignationem?... Quid igitur de bellis inter jam natos quereris cum nascituris nosti bella ipsa non defuisse, dum in matrum uteris bellasse fratres, scriptura testante, cognoscis? Cur ne ergo bellis jam nati carebunt, quibus antequam essent, minimi caruerunt?

12. In primis igitur dicturus de pace, illud, puto, fore supponendum, quod, ut sacri interpretes describunt, pax dicta est de pacto, quasi pactum faciens, vel a pactione mentis; quo sit, ut ubi unanimis ac conformis desit mentis tranquillitas, ibi pax ipsa vera desinat necesse...etc. Also the good effect of military discipline is suggested by the derivation castra—casta. Bella "wars" are bella "beautiful things" and peace is feminine and shrinks from war— these are other contentions of Rodericus.

# APPENDIX B

## A BIBLIOGRAPHY OF RODERICUS SANCIUS, BISHOP OF CALAHORRA

A list of the works of Rodericus Sancius is given by Antonio in his *Bibliotheca Hispana Vetus*, Book x, Chapter xi (vol. ii, p. 193 of the Roman edition of 1690). Although I have been able to make but few additions to his list in comparison with the whole, I think it worth while that this list should be printed, partly because Antonio's work is not very accessible, partly because I can claim to guide enquirers a little further on their way, and partly because no piece of evidence so illuminates the character of this genial bishop as a list of treatises from his pen, embracing in their scope such different subjects as religious mendicancy, education, sovereignty, Islam, the function of a castellan, the capture of Gibraltar, not to mention any of the numerous questions of contemporary politics, with which his speeches and his sermons freely deal. My researches in continental libraries have had to be conducted from this country. This makes me the more grateful to those in foreign lands who have helped me from the abundance of their knowledge, or by conducting enquiries on my behalf. I have given dates only when these seem beyond doubt.

1. 1467. Defensorium status Ecclesiastici contra querulos, aemulos, et detractores praelatorum et clericorum, divisum in decem tractatus. Antonio 591. *Vat. MS.* 4106.

2. De paupertate Christi et Apostolorum; et an Christus et Apostoli mendicarunt, et quo sensu dici potest eos mendicasse. Ibi denique deducitur praelatos et clericos modernos non deviare a vita Apostolica; licet obtineant propria, possessiones et praebendas distinctas, et quamquam segregatim in domibus propriis habitent, nihilominus eos vitam communem a sanctis patribus institutam ducere censendos fore.
Antonio 592. *Vat. MS.* 969.
Dedicated to Pope Paul II.

3. Liber, ubi agitur: an sine peccato fideles licite fugiant a locis ubi saevit pestis.
Antonio 593. *Vat. MS.* 4881. Milan, Ambr. Library.

# A BIBLIOGRAPHY OF RODERICUS SANCIUS 109

4. De monarchia orbis; in quo ostenditur apud Romanam pontificem residere veram orbis monarchiam.
Antonio 594. *Vat. MS.* 4881.
The treatise discusses the origin and distinctions between different kinds of authority. It touches upon imperial claims and those of modern kingdoms and principalities, especially Spain and France. It asserts the responsibility of monarchs not to the Emperor or their subjects, but to the Pope.

5. Defensorium hujus libri de monarchia orbis contra quosdam detractores.
Antonio 595. *Vat. MS.* 4881.
A defence of the Papal authority against Imperial attacks.

6. Apparatus, sive commenti super bullam Cruciatae indictae per Papam Pium contra perfidos Turcos.
Antonio 596.

7. ? 1466/7. Super commento bullae depositionis Regis Bohemiae per sanctissimum dominum Paul II publicatae.
Antonio 597. Venice, St Mark *Z. L.* CXCIV.
See Odericus Regnaldus, *Ann. Eccl.* vol. XVIII ad annum MCDLXVI, num. 25 and 26. Creighton, *Hist. of the Papacy.*

8. De remediis afflictae Ecclesiae militantis. In quo adhibentur remedia contra omnes persecutiones quas Ecclesia a domesticis et persecutoribus patitur.
Antonio 598.

9. De remediis afflictae Ecclesiae militantis adversus extrinsecas Turcorum persecutiones pressuras et angustias: et an generalis Synodus hoc tempore sit expediens et sufficiens remedium ad eas extirpandas. Demum ostenditur, quando et quomodo et ex quibus caussis generalia Concilia congregari debent. Rursus deducitur Romanum Pontificem habere in terris supremam authoritatem, foreque summum ordinarium tribunae ad levanda quaevis mala et incommoda ab ecclesia Dei.
Antonio 599. Padua. Library of the canons of St John.
Venice, St Mark *Z. L.* XC.
Dedicated to Cardinal Bessarion.

10. 1468. Speculum vitae humanae, de prosperis et adversis, dulcibus et amaris omnium statuum vitae mortalis, tam in statu spirituali quam temporali.
Antonio 600.
Jottings as to the responsibilities, duties, etc. of various highly placed officials. This book was often printed and proved most popular. See Proctor, *An index to the Early Printed Books in the British Museum*, passim. Hain, *Repertorium Bibliographicum*, Vol. II, Part 2, p. 223.

11. De regno dividendo et quando primogenitura sit licita.
Antonio 604. *Vat. MS.* 4881.

12. De pace et de bello et de necessitate et utilitate bellorum.
Antonio 605. *Vat. MS.* 4881. Venice, St Mark C. C. C. C. 166.
The dialogue is fully referred to above, Chap. I.

13. De eruditione puerorum.
Antonio 606. *Vat. MS.* 4881.

14. Liber confutatorius sectae et superstitionis Machometi et quorundam errorum in ea contentorum in quibusdam epistolis per quendam eloquentem oratorem missis perfido Turco.
Antonio 607.

15. 1467. Liber dialogi De auctoritate Rom. Pontificis et Generalium Conciliorum et de poena subtrahentium obedientiam a sede Apostolica et de remediis schismatum.
Antonio 608. *Vat. MS.* 4881. Padua. Lib. of St Benedict.
Dedicated to Pope Paul II.

16. Liber de castellanis et custodibus arcium et castrorum et de ducibus exercitus bellorum, et de eorum officio, et quales debeant esse.
Antonio 609.

17. Liber de questionibus ortholanis, introductus inter reverendum patrem Alphonsum Episcopum Burgensem ex una, et eundem Rodericum episcopum ex altera: quis sensus corporaliter altero sit utilior et praestantior et praesertim an visus sit excellentior et utilior auditu.
Antonio 610.

Hortolanis is a word constructed from hortus, "a garden," e.g., "garden talks," or from ὀρθρινός "early," e.g., "conversations of a morning."

18. Tractatus ad quendam religiosum Carthusiensem quando liceat religiosis curias principum sequi aut frequentare. Et quod aliquando expedit eos apud principes manere.
Antonio 611.

19. Tractatus de mysterio S. S. Trinitatis et an possit probari naturalibus rationibus.
Antonio 612.
Dedicated to Pius II.

20. Libellum ad beatissimum et clementissimum D.D. Paullum P.M. in quo testimoniis juris divini, naturalis et humani damnetur appellatio a sententia Romani Pontificis non bene, ut aiunt, informati ad eundem bene informatum. Adducuntur pro utraque parte rationes juris et auctoritates, tandem veritas multis testimoniis comprobatur, declaraturque quotuplex et qualis sit superioritas quae in appellatione requiritur.
Antonio 614. *Vat. MS.* 4167. Padua. Library of the Canons of St John.

21. Dialogus De remediis Schismatis.

Antonio 615. *Vat. MS.* 4002.

Dedicated to Garsias Henriquez, Bishop of Seville, member of the Privy Council of King John of Castille and Leon.

In the introduction the following light is thrown upon the origin of the book :

Nuper itaque, cum apud serenissimum principem Romanorum Imperatorem, aliquandiu demorarer, ad coenam me traxit invitum quidam Theodoricus juris professor insignis, vir arbitratu meo doctissimus, ac multarum rerum experientissimus. Ad mensam itaque nobis inter epulas confidentibus, ecce, ut puto, illius industria verbum prodiit de hac flebili Ecclesiae scissura, in qua re paullo ante egeram ipse verbum coram Caesarea majestate. Tangebat vir ille plurima in rebus ipsis sciscitans, quidnam caussae tantorum esset malorum, quidne remedium futurum videtur.

The conversation was then reduced to writing. The occasion of Roderic's visit was probably his mission from King John II to the Emperor.

22. Epistola ad doctissimum et religiosissimum virum Fr. Alphonsum de Palenguela, in qua agitur de multiplici onere et periculo Pontificalis dignitatis, et de ambitionis vitio, ac modernis abusibus praelatorum. Agitur etiam de modo pascendi gregem et de pluribus ad curam praesulatus spectantibus.

Antonio 616. *Vat. MS.* 3899.

23. Epistola lugubris et moesta, simul et consolatoria, de infelici expugnatione insulae Eubozae dictae Necropontis a perfido crucis Christi hoste Turcarum impiissimo principe et tyranno nuper inflicta, ad rever. P. ac sapientiss. dom. Bessarionem Cardinalem Sabinum et Patriarcham Constantinopolitanum.

Antonio 617. *Vat. MS.* 5869.

24. Historia Hispana. Antonio 619.

25. Oratio ad sanctissimum Papam Eugenium exparte serenissimi Regis Hispaniae (John II) contra factiones Basileensium. Ubi multa de devotione Regum Hispaniae ad Romanam ecclesiam.

Antonio 621. *Vat. MS.* 4881.

26. Oratio alia ad sacrum collegium Cardinalium super eadem materia. Antonio 622. *Vat. MS.* 4881.

27. Oratio ex parte ejusdem Regis Hispaniae ad Philippum Mariam Ducem Mediolani exhortatoria ad pacem Italiae et ut pure et simpliciter adhaeret dom. Eugenio et Basileensem factionem respueret. Antonio 623. *Vat. MS.* 4881.

28. Oratio ex parte ejusdem ad sereniss. Fredericum Imperatorem exhortatoria ad unitatem et pacem Ecclesiae et quod deceat Imperatores agere pro unione ac defensione Ecclesiae, inducens eundem Imperatorem ad puram adhaesionem dom. Eugenii et ad detestationem Basileensium.

*Antonio* 624. *Vat. MS.* 4881.

29. Oratio ad sereniss. Carolum Regem Franciae exparte ejusdem de laudibus ejusdem Caroli et gloriosae domus Franciae et Hispaniae, exhortatoria ad tollendas omnes occasiones dissidii inter utramque regiam domum. *Antonio* 625. *Vat. MS.* 4881.

30. Oratio ex parte sanctiss. dom. Nicolai Papae ad illustrissimum Ducem Burgundiae, ubi multa de devotione et favore ejusdem principis ad incrementa fidei.

*Antonio* 626. *Vat. MS.* 4881.

This is Duke Philip of Burgundy.

31. Oratio ad sanctiss. Papam Pium II nomine regis Hispaniae in praestatione obedientiae, ubi congratulatur de assumptione. Exhortatur ad exsterpationem Turcorum et multa de devotione Regum Hispaniae ad ecclesiam Romanam.

*Antonio* 627. *Vat. MS.* 4881.

Rex Hispaniae = Henry IV.

32. Oratio lugubris de obitu sereniss. Regis Joannis Hispaniae ad sereniss. Regem Carolum Franciae et de laudibus ejus Regis Johannis. *Antonio* 628. *Vat. MS.* 4881.

33. Oratio habita ad sanctissimum dominum Callistum, Papam secundum, in praestationem obedientiae et congratulatoria de assumptione: et multa pia opera adducit et singularem devotionem Regum Hispaniae ad sedem Apostolicam.

*Antonio* 629. *Vat. MS.* 4881.

Callistus II = Callistus III commonly so called.

34. Oratio habita Romae in nativitate primogenitae serenissimi Regis Hispaniarum et de causis gaudendi ob eundem natalem.

*Antonio* 630. *Vat. MS.* 4881.

35. Oratio ad sanctiss. Pium II de felici victoria et acquisitione civitatis de Gibraltar in stricto Oceani maris sitae, per capitaneos Regis Hispaniae et ibi multa de situ illius urbis et de utilitate fidei. *Antonio* 631. *Vat. MS.* 4881.

The capture took place 1462.

36. Oratio ad eundem Pontificem in conventione Mantuana ex parte Regis Hispaniae. Commendat dictum conventum pro expeditione contra Turcos. Exhortatur ad eundem expeditionem et pollicetur omnia auxilia ex parte ejusdem Regis. Exhortatur et ad pacem principum Christianorum.
Antonio 632. *Vat. MS.* 4881.

37. Sermo coram sanctissimo Nicholas Papa V in Dominica Passionis in Quadragesima. Antonio 633. *Vat. MS.* 4881.

38. Sermo coram sacro collegio Cardinalium in die St Thomae de Aquino. Antonio 634. *Vat. MS.* 4881.

39. Sermo coram sanctissimo domino Callisto in die ascensionis domini. Antonio 635. *Vat. MS.* 4881.

40. Sermo coram eodem in die Annunciationis B. Mariae Virginis. Antonio 636. *Vat. MS.* 4881.

41. Sermo coram sanctissimo domino Pio in die Sanctae Trinitatis. Antonio 637. *Vat. MS.* 4881.

42. Sermo coram sanctissimo domino Nicholas in die Apostolorum Petri et Pauli. Antonio 638. *Vat. MS.* 4881.

43. Sermo coram sanctiss. dom. Pio in die Pentecostis.
Antonio 639. *Vat. MS.* 4881.

44. Opuscula Roderici Episcopi Calagurritani, Castellani S. Angeli de Urbe et epistolae ejusdem ad quosdam doctissimos viros et illorum ad eum.
Antonio 639. *Vat. MS.* 4881. C. C. C. C. 166.

45. 1449. Sermo in passione domini factus Romae coram sanctissimo domino nostro Nicholas papa quinto ... anno MCCCCXLIX.
Not in Antonio. Koblenz Staatsarchiv. Abt 701 Nr 230.

# APPENDIX C

## ENGLISH VERSION OF PASSAGES QUOTED IN CHAPTER II

1. Nobility is conferred by the tenure of a Princedom. But it is often by patent, and often unexpressed. When by patent, as in the case of its being held in writing, or by the method of a personal concession, it is called "chartered" nobility, but when unexpressed, nobility is conferred indirectly, or without outward manifestation as in the case of anything conferred, which draws with it nobility, such as the rule of a Duchy or a County. For these enoble their possessors.

2. For always in the case of certain nations supreme sovereignty was in the people, and this is manifested as a provision of Divine Law. For when God created man, He gave to him sovereignty and dominion over other living beings; but He did not provide that one man should ever serve another. So, in the beginning, kings were not adopted by Divine Order, but from popular consent, and this, even after the fall of the Roman Empire, was preserved when Charles the Great was elected Augustus, by the Roman people, and anointed with Holy Oil by the Pope Leo. This popular sovereignty now-a-days has been transferred by the Gregorian Law to the 7 "Electors" of Germany. Similarly, when Chilperic was dethroned, because he was not capable of governing, the Franks substituted Pippin in a Pan-Celtic Conference; and when the descendants of Pippin had degenerated from their ancestors, they again elevated Odo, and shortly after his brother Robert, and then Hugh, the nephew of Robert, to the highest position. This is the Hugh who is commonly called Capet, from whom have sprung all those who, even now, govern the Frankish Dominions. And what has been said about these very great kings, to wit, the Roman and the Frankish, the same has been the practice in the case of their inferiors....So that I may be allowed to say that, according to Divine Law, he is a lawful Prince, who bases his rule on popular consent, which is just what Aristotle says. But he who rules over unwilling subjects is a tyrant, even though he is Caesar, elected by the Septemviri, or holds his position by any other provision of civil law. For this reason, when great kingdoms are in the first place

formed, not from the consent of the subjects, but by violence, St Augustine, in the 4th book of *The City of God*, rightly declared that a great crime has been committed.

3. It is necessary that a Monarchy should be elected and confirmed in the world, and should take its origin in Gaul, from the support and election of the Gallic people....It is necessary, according to my chief idea, to lay down in word and writing, that the most Christian Monarch, elected, approved, sustained and upheld by the Gallic people, should have, for ever, such authority throughout the world in temporal matters as St Peter has had, up to now, in spiritual.

4. For Law made by the Prince has the force of law, even if there has been no question of popular consent, but it is merely a matter of the Prince's will. For, in this connection, we must accept what is said on this point by Ulpian, in his first book: "Whatever pleases the Prince has the force of law," provided that, from this assumption, no absurdity follows, for who would think that Claudius' Edict should be regarded as a law, in which he warned the populace that nothing was such a specific for snake bite as the juice of a yew tree an incident which you will find in Suetonius on Claudius. Caesar is said, indeed, somewhere, to have declared that men should take for positive law whatever he might say, but this is an absurd utterance, and unworthy of the Prince, and undoubtedly brought upon him evil consequences. We ought to understand the above words concerning a prince who has a conscious purpose in declaring law, which conscious purpose has the force of law, and is called a constitution.

5. Kingdoms were founded with the purpose of preserving the existence of cities, for men understood that there was more protection and convenience in the ordering their affairs through the government of one wise man and monarch, than in the government of the whole people or a majority; because a wise man, relying on himself, or on the counsel of wise men, easily and quickly is able to take counsel for the common good, and follow up what he has rightly decided, since all obey him. But, in government by the many, on account of the diversity of men's opinions, and their natural tendency to differences, it may easily happen that their minds may be perverted into a diversity of opinion, and, in this way, either, in the end, nothing definite is determined, or if something is fixed too late, in the meantime the occasion and the chance of adequate performance will be slipping away.

6. There is no doubt that the King, who is chief founder, instructor, guardian, and defender of ecclesiastical interests, in his kingdom, not only by law should be able, but ought to take precaution and pains that the decrees and constitutions should be diligently observed, and with good faith, such as indubitably protect us from those things which we have declared undesirable.

7. Sometimes it is the people whom we ought to fear. Sometimes, if it is the practice of the State that most things are transacted by a senate, we should maintain ourselves as respectful citizens towards that. Sometimes it is individuals to whom the people's power, and power over the people is given.

8. For law, made by a Prince, necessity makes also. Thus, for no other reason do we create a Prince than that he should execute judgment, and declare law, as is clearly written....And it is very justly remarked by Accursius that the Centre of Gravity shifted from the people to the Senate, from the Senate to the Prince, by decentralization, progressively, slowly and step by step. What meaning does he attribute to the phrase "by decentralization"? In order that, he says, the state should be saved from the influence of one man. For the Senate was not a body sufficient to rule all the provinces. For this reason the Prince was set up, who should be lord of all, and should be the driving force behind all others by his authority.

9. Thus, according to Accursius, the powers of the people have been given to the Prince and committed to the Prince....Nor is there any other difference between the people and the Prince, except in that the people are bound by their own laws, but the Prince is exempt from his laws. But, just as the people are bound by their own laws, so they are also bound by the Prince's laws. Thus the people have bound, not only the Prince whom they have created to take their own place, but also themselves, by the laws of the Prince.

10. After those to whom, in this fashion, had been given supreme authority, had begun to act irrationally, and to issue prescriptions in the heat of their minds' passion, and after it appeared dangerous that the fortunes and life of the general public should be subordinated to the arbitrariness of one, in some cases, having turned out the kings, they drew up a Constitution. In others, keeping their kings, they submitted them to the control as it were of a constitution, in order to prevent the wild application of unlimited power by the control of law.

# APPENDIX D

## A BIBLIOGRAPHY OF WILLIAM POSTEL

To provide a new bibliography of the printed works of Postel is to undertake a task which those interested in French learning of the XVI century will not regard as profitless. That there are several earlier lists one is well aware[1], but for practical purposes a start is best made with that contained in Niceron, *Mémoires pour servir à l'histoire des hommes illustres dans la république des lettres*, tom. VIII, Paris 1729. This list was in turn most carefully edited by the Jesuit, Des Billons, for the treatise[2] which he published on Postel at Liège in 1773. Des Billons traced the existence in his day of many volumes. He also added about a dozen works to the list of Niceron. G. Weil, the most recent writer on the subject[3], is content to accept the list of Des Billons as one to work from, and only makes one or two additions to it. I have here followed his example, and the numerical order adopted is that of Des Billons. Books added by Weil or myself are distinguished by the addition of a letter to the numeral (e.g. 24*a*, 25*a*, 26*a*, etc.). Where possible I have inserted them in their right position chronologically. Work done carefully by scholars of a former generation imposes certain duties of piety upon successors, and I have copied another practice of Des Billons. It is a pleasant feature of his publication that the reader is enabled by it to trace the fate of actual copies of works which at the date of their publication played so important a part in their author's life. Rarely as the books of Postel figured in the auction rooms of the XVIII century, it is still more rarely that they do so now. I have, however, been

---

[1] For instance J. Simler, in his work on the Library of Gesner, gives a list of over thirty different books by Postel (Bibliotheca instituta et collecta primum a Conrado Gesnero : deinde in Epitomen redacta et novorum librorum accessione locupleta, tertio recognita et in duplum post priores editiones accreta per Josiam Simlarum, Tiguri, Christopherus Froschoverus, MDLXXXIII). There is a list of the French writings in *La Bibliothèque d'Antoine du Verdier Seigneur de Vaupuvas*, Lyons, MDLXXXV.

[2] *Nouveaux éclaircissements sur la vie et les ouvrages de Guillaume Postel*.

[3] De Guilielmi Postelli vita et indole ; Thesim proponebat Facultati Parisiensi G. Weil, Scholae Normalis olim alumnus. Lutetiae Parisiorum, apud Hachette Bibliopolam, MDCCCXCII.

able to chronicle the possession of some of them by certain famous British Libraries. British Libraries are not those in which they might be expected to abound. There has been no opportunity of consulting others in recent years, nor does the subject justify the labour which would be involved by doing so. What I have seen in British Libraries has helped me towards greater accuracy in re-publishing the list, and I shall be more than contented if some future worker on the subject outside these islands finds it of help to know what we possess within them. Twenty-six out of the sixty odd volumes I have not been able to trace. Perhaps it is merely a question of extending the search to other collections than those here dealt with before they are discovered. At the time of going to press I had not completed my examination of the Cambridge College Libraries. Those I had visited, with the exception of Trinity, proved disappointing.

ABBREVIATIONS.

1 Acton      Acton Library (in University Library, Cambridge).
2 Advoc      Advocates Library, Edinburgh.
3 Bod        Bodleian Library, Oxford.
4 B M        British Museum.
5 Dub        Library of Trinity College, Dublin.
6 U L C      University Library, Cambridge.

**1.** 1538. Linguarum duodecim characteribus differentium Alphabetum, Introductio, ac legendi modus longe facillimus. Linguarum nomina sequens proxime pagella offeret. Guilielmi Postel, Barentonii, diligentia.

Prostant Parisiis, apud Dionysium Lescuier.

Excudebat P. Vidovaeus Vernoliensis, Mense Martio, 1538.

B M 622 g 16, 684 g 21, 66 b 19, G 171 24;
U L C Aa 25 161; Bod; Dub Q KK 15.

4to. 75 pp.

**2.** 1538. Guilielmi Postelli, Baren. Doleriensis, de Originibus, seu de Hebraicae Linguae et Gentis Antiquitate; deque variarum Linguarum Affinitate, Liber. In quo ab Hebraeorum, Chaldaeorumve Gente traductas in toto Orbe Colonias, vocabuli Hebraici argumento, humanitatisque Authorum testimonio, videbis: Literas,

# A BIBLIOGRAPHY OF WILLIAM POSTEL

Leges, Disciplinasque omnes inde ortas cognosces: communitatemque notiorum Idiomatum aliquam cum Hebraismo esse.

B M 622 g 16², 684 g 21², 66 b 19³ ; U L C aa 25 16² ; Bod.
Prostant Parisiis, apud Dionysium Lescuyer. Excudebat Petrus Vidovaeus, Vernoliensis, vigesima septima Martii. Anno a partu virginis 1538.
4to. 57 pp.

3. 1538. Grammatica Arabica. Guilielmus Postellus lectori: Nequid nostri consilii ignores, candide lector, quum characterum difficultate in sculptis Tabulis multos esse perterritos viderem, quod essent difficiles et male formati, volui loco illorum Quaternionum hic inserere Grammaticam typis excussam ut, quos difficultate abegerat, facilitate et pulchritudine revocet. Vale.
Veneunt Parisiis apud Petrum Gramorsum.

B M 622 g 16, 66 b 19; U L C Aa 25 16³; Dub ee c 2¹.
4to. 44 pp.
This treatise was considered by its author as a supplement to be bound up with No. 1 after the first four gatherings (quaterniones) of that treatise.

4. 1540. Descriptio Syriae. B M 793 c 7.
Parisiis apud Hieronymum Gormontium.
Bod ; Dub.
8vo. 21 pp.

*Later edition.*
1737. In Tempe Helvetica, tom. II, p. 349. Tiguri 1737. 29 pp.
B M 95 c 2; Bod; Dub dd hh 47⁴.

5. 1541. De Magistratibus Atheniensium Liber singularis. Parisiis, ex officina Michaelis Vascosani.
B M 802 f 8¹; U L C z 11 9; Bod; Advoc; Dub 55 n 81.
4to. 64 leaves.

*Later editions.*
n.d. ? 1543/1551 Basle.
B M 878 g 6², 244 a 25, 584 b 28; Dub pp mm 36³.
151 + 14 pp.

1635. Leyden 8vo.
Leyden 24mo. John Balesdens, Ex officina Johannis Maire.
B M 802 a 30; U L C l+ 13 9 (G);
Acton e 24 6; Bod; Dub v bb 3.
1645. Leyden 24mo.
B M 9025 a 14; Dub Frag. b 12 38.

1691. Leyden 8vo. 2 parts. B M 9039 aaa 24.
Leyden, in Graec. antiq. tom. v. folio pp. 27.
B M 1709 b 4; U L C z 7 31. PP⁺ 1 143;
Bod; Dub Frag E 2 5; Advoc.

6. 1543. Alcorani, seu Legis Mahometi, & Evangelistarum Concordiae Liber, in quo de calamitatibus Orbi Christiano imminentibus tractatur: additus est libellus de universalis Conversionis, judiciive tempore; et, intra quot annos sit expectandum, conjectatio, ex divinis ducta Authoribus, veroque proxima. Parisiis, apud Petrum Gramorsum. B M 696 b 17²; Advoc.
8vo. 123 pp.

7. 1543. De Rationibus Spiritus Sancti; Libri duo. Guilielmo Postello Barentonio authore. Parisiis, apud Petrum Gramorsum.
B M 4374 a 2; U L C; C 12 42¹; Acton e 46 11².
8vo. 53 leaves.

8. 1543. Sacrarum Apodixeon, seu Euclidis Christiani Lib. duo. Parisiis. Excudebat ipsi Authori Petrus Gramorsus. 1543.
B M 696 b 17¹; U L C a 12 42²; Acton e 46 11¹.
8vo. 56 leaves.

9. *n.d.* 1543? Quatuor Librorum, de Orbis Terrae Concordia, primus. Guilielmo Postello Barentonio, Math. prof. regio authore, Parisiis. Excudebat Petrus Gramorsus.
B M 847 d 5; U L C c 12 42³; Bod; Advoc.
8vo. 144 leaves.

10. *n.d.* 1544. De Orbis Terrae Concordia Libri IV. No place. No date. ? Basileae, ex officina Johannis Oporini. 1544. *Folio. 456 pp.* (*Niceron and Vogt*). *447 pp.* (*Des Billons*).
It is 447 pp. in all copies I have seen, though the last page is numbered by mistake 427.
B M c 76 d 12, 11 b 4, U L C; F⁺ 9 24,
G 9 14; Acton b 47 41, b 46 87; Bod.
Dub. cc b 26; Advoc.

11. *n.d.* 1547. Absconditorum a constitutione Mundi Clavis, qua mens humana, tam in divinis, quam in humanis, pertinget ad interiora velaminis aeternae Veritatis.

*Later editions.*
? 1552. Paris. ? Basileae, ex off. Oporini. 16mo.
? 1555. 12mo. B M Paris. ? 1555. 8vo. Bod. Paris.

# A BIBLIOGRAPHY OF WILLIAM POSTEL 121

1646. 16mo. Amsterdam, Janssen. Editore A. Frank de Monte S. (Frankeberg) Una cum appendice Pro Pace Religionis Christianae.
B M 847 a 16, U L C; KKK 381; Acton e 46 12; Dub cc p. 33.

**12.** *n.d.* 1547. ΠΑΝΘΕΝΩΣΙΑ, sive Compositio omnium Dissidiorum, circa aeternam Veritatem aut Verisimilitudinem versantium, quae non solum inter eos, qui hodie Infidelium, Judaeorum, Haereticorum, et Catholicorum nomine vocantur, orta sunt et vigent, sed jam ab admissis per peccatum, circa nostrum intellectum, tenebris fuere inter Ecclesiae peculiaris et communis Membra. Scriptore Elia Pandocheo. Tubae penultimae stridor.

No place or date mentioned but author's word for 1547 and Operinus at Basle.

U L C Bb+ 15 24² A+ 8ª 49 (F); Dub PP mm 36.
8vo. 143 pp.

**13.** *n.d.* 1547. De Nativitate Mediatoris ultima, nunc futura, & toti Orbi Terrarum, in singulis ratione praeditus, manifestanda, opus: in quo totius Naturae obscuritas, origo, creatio, ita cum sua causa illustratur, exponiturque, ut vel pueris sint manifesta, quae in Theosophiae et Filosophiae Arcanis hactenus fuere. Autore Spiritu Christi: Exscriptore Gulielmo Postello, Apostolica professione Sacerdote.

Basiliae, ex officina Johannis Oporini (but no place nor date mentioned).

B M 479 a 18, 225 c 33; U L C; Acton d 46 309; Bod; Dub BB hh 30; Advoc.
4to. 187 pp.

**14.** 1548. Candelabri Typici, in Mosis Tabernaculo, jussu divino, expressi, brevis ac dilucida interpretatio. Venetiis.
8vo.

**15.** 1551. De Etruriae Regionis, quae prima in Orbe Europaeo habitata est, Originibus, Institutis, Religione & Moribus, & imprimis de Aurei Saeculi Doctrina & Vita praestantissima, quae in Divinationis sacrae usu posita est, Commentatio. Florentiae.

B M 663 b 4, 1057 h 31, 175 d 19; U L C; Acton d 24 125; Bod; Dub N 7 36; Advoc.
4to. 251 pp.

*Later edition.*

1725. Graeve and Burman. Thesaurus antiq. Italiae., tom. VIII pars I.

B M Circ 18b; U L C Bb 7 26; Dub QQ b 10; Advoc.

**16. 1551.** Les Raisons de la Monarchie, et quelz moyens sont necessaires pour y parvenir ; la ou sont compris en brief les très admirables, et de nul jusques aujourd'huy tout ensemble considerez Privileges et Droicts, tant divins, celestes, comme humains, de la Gent Gallicque et des Princes par icelle esleuz et approuvez. Par Guillaume Postel. Moriar ut suscip. Avec Privilege pour dix ans.

[At the end of volume] Imprimé à Paris, le quinziesme jour de May, mil cinq cens cinquante et ung.

8vo. 48 pp. Reprinted Tours the same year.

**17. 1552.** Abrahami Patriarchae Liber Jezirah, sive formationis Mundi, Patribus quidem, Abrahami tempora praecedentibus, revelatus, sed ab ipso etiam Abrahamo expositus Isaaco, et per Prophetarum manus posteritati conservatus ; ipsis autem 72 Mosis Auditoribus, in secundo divinae Veritatis loco, hoc est, in Ratione, quae est posterior Authoritati, habitus. Vertebat ex Hebraeis, & Commentariis illustrabat 1551, ad Babylonis ruinam & corrupti Mundi finem, Guil. Postellus Restitutus. Parisiis.

16mo. 40 pp. U L C c⁺ 13 28 ; Dub E o 12.

**18. 1552.** Restitutio rerum omnium conditarum, per manum Eliae Prophetae terrabilis, ut fiat in toto mundo conversio perfecta, & maxime inter Judaeos. Interprete ex Hebraeis Guil. Postello. Parisiis. U L C c⁺ 13 28.

16mo. 31 pp. Often, but not always, bound with 17.

**19. 1552.** Liber de Causis, seu de Principiis et originibus Naturae utriusque : in quo ita de aeterna rerum veritate agitur ut & Authoritate & Ratione, Non tantum ubivis particularis Dei Providentia, sed & animorum et corporum immortalitas ex ipsius Aristotelis verbis recte intellectis et non detortis demonstretur clarissime. Parisiis.

16mo. 36 sheets. B M 1017 6 6 ; Bod.

**20. 1552.** Liber de ultimo Judicio & de Causis Naturae utriusque.

No place, no date given.

16mo.

**21. 1552.** Vinculum Mundi, compendio expositum, in quo basis earum rationum exponitur, quibus veritas Articulorum Fidei Christianae aut probatur, aut defenditur. Parisiis, in Quadragesima, dictabat Auditorum suorum humanitati, in Babylonis ruinam

# A BIBLIOGRAPHY OF WILLIAM POSTEL 123

Guilielmus Postellus, 1552, ad corrupti Mundi finem. Prostant Exemplaria sub Ciconiis (apud Sebastianum Nivelium) in via Jacobaea.
4to. 8 pp.

**22. 1552.** Eversio falsorum Aristotelis Dogmatum, Auctore D. Justino Martyre: Guilielmo Postello, in tenebrarum Babylonicarum dispulsionem, interprete. Parisiis.
16mo. 168 pp.

**23. 1552.** L'Histoire memorable des Expeditions depuys le Déluge, faictes par les Gauloys ou Françoys depuys la France jusques en Asie, ou en Thrace, & en l'orientale partie de L'Europe: & des commodites ou incommodites des divers chemins pour y parvenir & retourner; le tout en brief ou Epitome, pour monstrer avec quelz moyens L'Empire des Infideles peult et doibt par eulx estre deffaict.

[At the end] L'Apologie de la Gaule contre les malevoles Escripvains, qui d'icelle ont mal ou négligement escript; & en après les très anciens droicts du Peuple Gallicque & de ses princes. Par Guillaume Postel. Paris. Sebastien Nivelle.

16mo. 95 leaves.
B M 688 a 21, 285 a 44.

**24. 1552.** De Phoenicum (Foenicum) Literis, seu de prisco Latinae & Graecae Linguae Charactere, ejusque antiquissima Origine et Usu, ad Carolum Cardinalem & Principem Lotharingium, Primarium Galliae Antistatem, Commentatiuncula. Guilielmo Postello, Barentonio, Authore. Parisiis, apud Martinum Juvenem.

B M 622 a 7 (2), 672 a 29 (4), 236 g 34, G 16733 (1);
U L C N+ 13 20G; Bod; Dub ss o 34; Advoc.
8vo. 51 leaves. Two charts of oriental characters should be included.

*Later edition.*
1740. Havercampus.
B M 673 e 20; Bod; Advoc.

**24a. 1552.** De Universitate liber, in quo astronomiae doctrinaeve coelestis compendium terrae aptatum, & secundum coelestis influxus ordinem praecipuarumque Originum rationem totus orbis Terrae quatenus innotuit, cum Regnorum temporibus exponitur. Sed ante omneis alias orbis parteis TERRA SANCTA summo, hoc est amplissimo, compendio describitur cui Gallia ob primarium orbis nomen et jus substituitur, eo quod ambae toti orbi legem sunt daturae.

## 124 A BIBLIOGRAPHY OF WILLIAM POSTEL

Guilielmo Postello Restituto in Regni Evangelici assertionem authore.
E typographia Ioannes Gueullartii.    U L C Bb⁺ 3 36 ; Bod.
1522. 60 leaves.

*Later editions.*
1553.    Dub. L Ee 9 ; Advoc.
1563. Parisiis, apud Martinum Juvenem.    B M 568 d 29.
4to. See below No. 46.
1635. Leyden ex officina Johanni Maire.
     U L C ; Acton e 24 612 ; Bod ; Dub QQ pp 5 ;
1685. Leyden.    B M 569 a 5, 793 a 3, 224 a 40.
See however below No. 44.

**25.** 1552. Tabulae in Astronomiam, in Arithmeticam, & in Musicam Theoreticam. Parisiis. Guil. Cavillat.    B M 17 h 1 (2).

**25a.** Tabulae variae.    B M 17 h 1 (3).
(Imagines coeli—one undated, one 1553.)
In Arati Solensis phaenomena.
Tabula aeternae ordinationis.

**26.** 1552. La Loy Salique, Livret de la première humaine vérité : là ou sont en brief les origines et authoritez de la Loy Gallique, nommée communement Salique, pour monstrer à quel poinct fauldra nécessairement en la Gallique République venir, & que de ladicte République sortira ung Monarche temporel. Par Guil. Postel.    B M 688 a 20, 882 a 3, 229 a 36.
Paris. 16mo. 47 leaves.

*Later editions.*
1559. Lyons.
1780. Paris. 92 pp.    B M 705 a 17, C 22a 51 (on vellum).

**26a.** 1552. A Broadsheet.
Resolution Eternelle destinée au Roy et peuple très-chrestien pour obtenir la vraye et finale victoire.

**27.** 1552. Protevangelion, sive de Natalibus Jesu-Christi et ipsius Matris Virginis Mariae Sermo Historicus, divi Jacobi Minoris, consobrini et fratris Domini Jesu, Apostoli primarii, & Episcopi Christianorum primi Hierosolymis. Accedit Evangelica Historia, quam scripsit Beatus Marcus, Petri Apostolorum Principis Discipulus & Filius, & primus Alexandriae Episcopus ; una cum vita

# A BIBLIOGRAPHY OF WILLIAM POSTEL 125

ejusdem Marci Evangelistae. Haec omnia in lucem edita studio Theodori Bibliandri. Basileae, ex officina Johannis Oporini.

8vo. This is the famous pseudo-gospel of St James the Less.

*Later editions.*
1564. Basle. M. Neander. See: U L C F⁺ 12 26 (Bibliander).
1570. Strassburg.

**28.** 1553. De Originibus, seu de varia, & potissimum Orbi Latino ad hanc diem incognita, aut inconsiderata Historia, quum totius Orientis, tum maxime Tartarorum, Persarum, Turcarum, & omnium Abrahami et Noachi alumnorum origines, & mysteria Brachmanum retegente: quod ad gentium, literarumque, quibus utuntur, rationes attinet: ex Libris Noachi & Hanochi, totiusque avitae traditionis, a Mosis alumnis ad nostra tempora servatae, & Chaldaicis literis conscriptae, Guilielmus Postellus posteritati eruit, exposuit, & proposuit.
Basileae, per Joannem Oporinum.
[At the end of the Volume] 1553 mense septimo a Januario primo.

B M 580 a 1², 224 a 13; U L C P 6 21; Acton d 24 344; Bod; Dub PP mm 36¹.

8vo. 135 pp.

**29.** 1553. Sibyllinorum Versuum, Virgilio in quarta Bucolicorum Versuum Ecloga transcriptorum, Ecfrasis, Commentarii instar, Guilielmo Postello Authore.
Parisiis, e Typographia Joannis Gueullartii, 1553.
4to. 6 pp.

**30.** 1553. Descriptions des Gaules, autrement la Carte Gallicane par G. Postel.
Paris. 1553. Folio.

**31.** 1553. Signorum Coelestium vera Configuratio, aut Asterismus, stellarumve per suas imagines aut configurationes dispositio, & in eum ordinem, quam illis Deus praefixerat, restitutio, & significationum expositio; sive Coelum repurgatum & apotelesmate summo determinatum. Nam per significationem stellarum videbitur quid sit in totius mundi imperiis futurum.
Parisiis. Hier. Gourmontius. 1553.

B M 8561 c 47, 13 a 10; Bod; Dub L ee 9³.

4to. 20 leaves.

*Later editions.*
1636. Leyden. John Balesdens ex officina Johannis Maire. As sequel to his Cosmographica disciplina. U L C ; Acton e 24 6. 16mo.
1661. Leyden. 16mo.

**32.** 1553. Les tres-merveilleuses Victoires des Femmes du nouveau Monde, et comme elles doibvent à tout le Monde par Raison commander et même à ceulx qui auront la Monarchie du Monde vieil. Par Guillaume Postel. A ma Dame Margarite de France. Paris. Jean Gueullart. B M 688 a 29$^1$.
16mo. 56 leaves. Also counterfeit edition in 8vo. 92 pp.
B M 16522.
Often bound up with the following.
B M 224 b 3$^1$.

**33.** 1553. La Doctrine du Siécle doré, ou de l'evangélike Regne de Jesus Roy des Roys. Paris. Jean Ruelle. 1553.
B M G 16522.
16mo. 27 pp.

*Later edition.*
1869. Turin. Gay et fils. Ed. Brunet. B M 4379 dd 21.

**34.** 1553. Des Merveilles des Indes & du nouveau Monde, ou est monstré le lieu du Paradis Terrestre. Par Guil. Postel. Paris. Jean Ruelle.
16mo. 96 pp.

**34***a*. 1553. Apologia pro Serveto Villanovamo, etc.
16mo.

*Later edition.*
1748. Mosheim, in Ketzergeschichte. U L C 7 1 54.
pp. 466.

**35.** 1553. Description & Charte de la Terre-Saincte, qui est la propriété de Jesus Christ, pour y voir sa pérégrination, & pour inciter ses très Chrestiens Ministres à la recouvrer, pour y replanter son Empire.
A très Chrestienne princesse Catharine de Medicis de sang Etrusque, Royne de la Gaule. Paris. Jean Ruelle.
B M 1016 a 8 ; U L C u$^+$ d 7 (G), 7 1 54.
16mo. 108 pp. See below No. 44 and above No. 24*a*.

**36.** Vraye et brieve Description de la Guerre et Ruyne de Troyes, anciennement descripte par Darès Phrygius, & commentée par Guillaume Postel.

37. 1553. Des Merveilles du Monde, & principalement des admirables choses des Indes & du nouveau Monde; Histoire extraicte des escripts très dignes de foy, tant de ceulx qui encore sont à présent au dict pays, comme de ceulx qui, encore vivants, peu paravent en sont retournez; & y est aussi monstré le lieu du Paradis terrestre. Paris. Ruelle. 1553.
16mo.

38. 1554. Guilielmi Postelli, Regii in Academia Viennensi Linguarum peregrinarum et Mathematum Professoris, de Linguae Phoenicis, sive Hebraicae, excellentia, & de necessario illius & Arabicae penes Latinos usu, Praefatio, aut potius Loquutionis, humanaeve Perfectionis Panegyris. Viennae Austriae opera Michaelis Cummermanni. A°. 1554.
4to.

39. 1555. Le prime nove del altro Mondo, cioe, l'admirable historia & non meno necessaria & utile da esser letta & intesa da ogniuno, che stupenda, intitulata, la Vergine Venetiana, parte vista, parte provata & fidelissimamente scritta per Guilielmo Postello, primogenito della Restitutione & spirituale Padre di esse vergine.

Jeremiae 31. *Creavit* Dominus Jhovah novum super terram.

Appresso del Autore. 1555.

Venice (so said by Flaccus Illyricus). B M 1071 K 18.
8vo. 80 pp.

40. 1556. Il libro della Divina Ordinatione, dove si tratta delle cose miraculose, lequali sono state, & sino al fine Hanno da essere in Venetia, & principalmente la causa, per laquele Iddio fin qui habbi havuto piu cura di Venetia, che di tutto quanto il Mondo insieme : per Guilielmo Postello.

In Padova, per Gratioso Perchacino, 1556.
8vo. 28 pp.

41. 1556. Epistola Guilielmi Postelli ad C. Schwenckfeldium, cum praefatione M. Mathiae Flaccii Illyrici. 1 Timoth. 4. Obtestor ego coram Deo & Domino Jesu Christo, etc. Praedica sermonem, insta tempestive, intempestive argue, increpa, hortare cum omni lenitate & doctrina. Nam erit tempus, cum sanam doctrinam non sustinebunt. (End of volume.)

Jenae. Excudebat Christianus Rhodius, anno 1556.
8vo. 7 pp.

*Later edition.*

1700. Halae Magdeburgicae. 8vo. (In Observationes selectae ad rem Litterariam spectantes, pp. 358, 368. T. I.)

**41a.** 1557. Appendix ad Johannis Carionis mathematici chronicorum Libros tres. Parisiis.
16mo.

**42.** 1560. (α) De la Républic des Turcs, et là ou l'occasion s'offrera, des Meurs & Loy de tous Muhamadistes. Par Guillaume Postel Cosmopolite. A Poitiers, par Enguilbert de Marnes. Avec privilege du Roy. 1560. (On verso of frontispiece: Achevé d'imprimer le 9 Decembre 1559, in 4to.)
4to. 127 pp.

1560. (β) Histoire et considération de l'Origine, Loy et Coustume des Tartares, Persiens, Arabes, Turcs, et tous autres Ismaelites ou Muhamediques dits par nous Mahometains ou Sarrazins. A Poitiers, de l'Imprimerie d'Enguilbert de Marnes. 1560. Avec privilege du Roy.

BM 281 G 9 10, 1436 h 1; U L C; Acton D 42 74; Bod; Dub PP f 19.

4to. 57 pp.

1560. (γ) La tierce partie des Orientales Histoires, ou est exposée la condition, puissance, et revenu de l'Empire Turquesque: avec toutes les Provinces et Pays, généralement depuis 950 ans ça par tous Ismaelites conquis. Pour donner, avec telle connoissance, vouloir & moyens de tels pays & richesses conquérir aux Princes et Peuples Tres-Chrestiens & aisnés au Droict du Monde. Par Guillaume Postel Cosmopolite. A Poitiers, par Enguilbert de Marnes 1560. Avec privilege du Roy.
4to. 90 pp.

These three are separate treatises, but are generally bound up together. Fifteen years later a new edition appeared under the title:

(**1575**) Histoires Orientales & principalement des Turkes, ou Turchikes, & Schitiques ou Tartaresques & autres, qui en sont descendues, Oeuvre pour la tierce fois augmenté et divisée en trois parties, par Guillaume Postel Cosmopolite, deux fois de la retourne et veritablement informé; avec une nomenclature de la langue Turque et avec l'Indice des choses les plus memorables y contenus. Paris, de Marnes et Cavellat. 1575.

BM 1313 a 4, 688 a 23, 780 b 40.

In 16mo, also in 8vo. 374+84 pp.
There is also another edition.

1565. Poitiers.     BM G 4216.

**43. 1561.** Cosmographicae Disciplinae Compendium, in suum finem, hoc est, ad Divinae Providentiae certissimam demonstrationem conductum. Addita est rerum toto Orbe gestarum Synopsis. Item, quot quantaeque Christianarum Gentium Nationes, nobis hactenus incognitae in universo sint, quae a nostro Orbe lumen Evangelii restitutum iri credunt. Gulielmo Postello Authore. Cum locuplete rerum & verborum memorabilium Indice.
Basileae, per Johannem Oporinum 1561.
B M 568 e 31 ; Dub EE g 221 ; Bod.
4to. 79 pp. With charts.

*Later editions.*
1635 Leyden. Ed. John Maire. 2 vols.
1636 „ „ „ „
U L C ; Acton e 24 6 ; Bod ; Dub FA B 12 25.

**44. 1562.** La Concordance des quatres Evangiles, ou Discours de la Vie de notre Seigneur Jesus-Christ, avec l'ordre des Evangiles et Epîtres, qui se disent dans l'Eglise au long de l'année : ensemble le Calendrier, ou ordre des temps, depuis la création du Monde, pour tout jamais restitué & corrigé, comme il appert en la raison d'iceluy Calendrier. Plus une brieve Descriptio de la Terre-Sainte, avec sa Carte. B M 1016 a 8.
Paris. W. Guillard & Amaury Warencove. 1562.
16mo. 440 + 333 + 108 pp.
See above No. 24*a* and 35, and below, No. 46.

**45. 1563.** L'unique Moyen de l'accord des Protestants, appellez en France Huguenots, & des Catholiques ou Romains & Papistes, proposé avec raison. Lyons 1563.

**46. 1563.** Guil. Postelli de Universitate Liber, in quo Astronomiae, Doctrinaeve coelestis Compendium, Terrae aptatum ; & secundum coelestis influxus ordinem, praecipuarumque Originum rationem, totus Orbis Terrae, quatenus innotuit, cum Regnorum temporibus, exponitur, etc. Secunda aeditio. Parisiis. Martinus Juvenis. 1563. B M 568 d 29.
4to. 43 pp. and charts.
Des Billons had not apparently seen No. 24*a*.

**47. 1563.** De raris & Posteritati notandis Historiis, & de admirandis rebus, quae a quinquaginta annis contiguerunt usque ad annum Salutis 1553 ; & quae inde ad annum 1583 contingent.

**48. 1571.** Divinationis, sive divinae summaeque Veritatis Discussio, qua constat, quid sit de clarissima inter Christianos & Ismaëlitas Victoria futurum, atque ubinam Gentium & locorum contingere debeat, & quamobrem. Paris 1571.

12mo. 66 pp. and chart.
B M 1407 a 25, 1407 a 24 ; Bod.

**49. 1572.** De Stella Peregrina, quae anno 1572 apparere coepit, Clariss. Virorum Corn. Gemmae Louvaniensis. 4to. Germani et Guliel. Postelli Barentani Galli, ex Philosophiae naturalis, mysticaeque Theologiae penetralibus deprompta judicia.

14 pp.
B M 8560 c 47, K 9 53$^5$, 7 13 26$^5$.

**49a.** Des histoires orientales. See above No. 42.
U L C Syn. 8 57 137 ; Bod.

**50. 1576.** Vers François, au nombre de cinquante, fort mauvais de Guillaume Postel Cosmopolite en faveur des Recherches des monnoyes, poix & nombres anciens & modernes du Sieur Garrault, imprimés à la tête du Livre de cet Auteur. Paris. 1576.
8vo.

**51.** Quaedam ex pietate insignis & eruditione viri D. G. Postelli Literis ad Corbinellum.

See pp. 65-75. Dantis Aligerii, praecellentiss. Poetae de vulgari eloquentia Libri duo, nunc primum, ad vetusti et unici scripti Codicis exemplar, editi, ex libris Corbinelli, ejusdemque adnotationibus illustrati. Parisiis **1577.**
8vo.

**52. 1579.** Les premiers Eléments d'Euclide Chrestien, pour raison de la Divine & eternelle vérité demonstrer; escrits en vers par Guillaume Postel, dit Rorisperge, Doyen des lectures du Roy. Paris.
8vo. Cf. No. 8.

**53.** *n.d.* Axiochus, a Platonic translation.
No place mentioned.

**54.** Chavae, seu Evae Prophetiae, e Raziele, ex libro Bahir, cum Apologia de ratione tanti Mysterii.

This only known through the list of works published in Frankeberg's La Clé des choses cachées. Very doubtful if it was ever printed.

**55.** Receuils des Prophéties de tous les plus célebres Peuples du Monde, par lequel il se voit comment le Roy des François, ou

bien celui qui entre tous les Princes d'Occident est le plus renommé, doit tenir la Monarchie de tout le Monde.
Probably not printed.

56. Les Prophéties, par Rustician recolligées & imprimées en Italien à Venize.
Doubtful if printed.

57. L'Arbre, dict Ilam, des secrets Mystires, imprimé en Hébrieu.

58. Tabula Restitutionis omnium.     B M 17 h 1 (5).

59. Petition directed to 'Nosseigneurs de Parlement' asking that the Faculty of Paris should be instructed to examine Postel's books and pass what they considered suitable.     B M 17 h 1 (4).

# CHRONOLOGICAL TABLE

It may prove useful to set down a few important dates of the period covered by the Essays in this book.

1404 Birth of Rodericus Sancius
1409 Council of Pisa
1414 Council of Constance
1431–49 Council of Basle
1438 Council of Florence Gemistos Plethon at Florence
1453 Capture of Constantinople by Mohammed II
1458 Election of Pius II
1460 (about) Foundation of the Roman Academy
1461 Louis XI ascends the throne of France
1464 Paul II elected Pope
1466 Colet born
1467 Erasmus born
1471 *Rodericus Sancius dies*
1480 Sir Thomas More born
1483 Death of Louis XI. Accession of Charles VIII
1485–98 Italian visits of Sellinge, Linacre, Grocyn, Latimer and Colet
1485 Accession of Henry VII
1492 *Birth of Alciat*
1509 Accession of Henry VIII *Birth of Duaren*
1510 *Birth of William Postel*
1513 Machiavelli's "Prince" written
1514 "Epistolae Obscurorum Virorum," Vol. I published
1515 Accession of Francis I
1516 More's "Utopia" published
1517 Luther's Theses published at Wittenberg "Epistolae Obscurorum Virorum," Vol. II
1522 *Birth of Cujas*
1527 *Birth of Doneau* Sack of Rome
1529 Fall of Wolsey
1531 Henry VIII declared Supreme Head of the Church *Birth of Brisson*
1533 *Birth of Connan*
1534 Foundation of the Society of Jesus
1535 More beheaded
1536 Calvin at Geneva
1545 Opening of the Council of Trent
1547 Accession of Edward VI Accession of Henry II
1549 *Birth of Denys Godfrey*
1550 *Death of Alciat*
1553 Accession of Queen Mary
1555 Abdication of the Emperor Charles V
1558 Accession of Elizabeth Accession of Francis II
1559 *Death of Duaren*
1560 Accession of Charles IX *Birth of Sully*
1563 The Thirty-Nine Articles Council of Trent closes finally
1571 Battle of Lepanto
1572 The Massacre of St Bartholomew
1574 Accession of Henry III Death of Archbishop Parker
1576 Bodin publishes "Six Livres de la République"
1577 Drake's voyage round the world
1581 *Death of William Postel*
1587 The Execution of Mary Queen of Scots
1588 The Spanish Armada Marlowe's "Tamburlaine"
1589 Death of Catharine de Medici

1590 *Death of Cujas*
     Battle of Ivry
     *Birth of Emerich Crucé*
1591 *Death of Doneau*
     *Death of Brisson*
     Foundation of Trinity College, Dublin
1592 Death of Parma
1594 "La Satire Ménipée"
     Hooker's "Ecclesiastical Polity"
1598 Treaty of Vervins

1598 Edict of Nantes
1603 Accession of James I
1607 Incident at Donauwörth
1609 Catholic Union formed
1610 Murder of Henry IV
1618 Outbreak of Thirty Years' War
1622 *Death of Denys Godfrey*
1641 *Death of Sully*
1648 Treaty of Westphalia
     *Death of Emerich Crucé*

# INDEX

Abbreviators, papal 6, 11
Abelard 7
Academy, Roman 9, 10, 11, 24
Acton, Lord 16, 51, 65
Alciat, events in life of 28, 35, 36
  ,,  tract on duelling 28
  ,,  views of 29–30
Alençon, Duc d', death of 33
Amalfi, Duke of 3
Amphictyonic Councils 100
Ancona 3, 4
Angelo, St, Castle of 3, 11
Angers 43, 71
Animus and anima 46, 53
Anselm 43
Antiquarianism, revived at Rome 9
Antonio 1, 108
Arabic type 62
Arguments from nature 17–19
Aristotle 7, 8, 19, 29, 40
Armstrong, Mr E. 26

Bacon, Francis 61
Balch 92
Barbo, Cardinal Marco 2
Barbo, Pietro, Pope Paul II 2
Bartholus 27
Basil the Macedonian, the Emperor 97
Basle 55, 57, 59
Baudrillart 89, 104
Bayle 9
Beaumont and Fletcher 87, 93
Berkeley, Sir Robert 32
Berosus 49
Besançon 30, 57
Bessarion, Cardinal 8, 24
Beza 40, 66
Bibliothèque Nationale, Sully's Manuscript in 84
Biragues, René de 93
Bismarck, Otto von 20, 69
Bobadilla 58
Bodin 46, 85, 100
Bois-rosé 72
Bomberg, Daniel 42
Bressiaeus 61
Brisson, views on Kingship 32
Bucer 41
Buonacursi, Filippo, *see* Callimachus Experiens
Burleigh 87

Cabbala, The 42, 46
Callimachus Experiens (Filippo Buonacursi) 10
Calvin, John 39, 67, 96
Cambridge, Regius Professorship of Civil Law 35
*Cambridge Modern History* 65
Canalisation 94
Canisius 58
Canterbury, Christ Church Priory 1
Capet, House of 29
Cecil, Lord Robert 65, 102
Cecil, William, *see* Burleigh
Chamberland, Albert 65
Charlemagne 29, 94
Charles (I), king of Sweden 79
Charles (VII), king of France 27
Charles (IX), king of France 93, 94
"Civilians," French, *see* Chapter II
  ,,  lack of uniformity among 26
  ,,  lack of subservience 28
  ,,  detachment of 28, 29, 36
  ,,  estimate of their influence 36–37
Clark, J. W. 12
Conciliar movement 6
Connan, education of 34
  ,,  views on the theory of government 34–36
Copernicus 104
Corpus Christi College, Cambridge iv, 1
Creighton, Mandell, *History of the Papacy* 1, 8, 9
Crichton, The Admirable 46
Crucé, Emerich, *see* Chapter V *passim* 86
  ,,  life 92
  ,,  views on protection 93
  ,,  on canalisation 94
  ,,  on piracy 95
  ,,  on education 96
  ,,  on religion 96
  ,,  on toleration 97
  ,,  on a World Congress 99, 100
  ,,  on precedence 100
Cujas, *see* Chapter II *passim* 39
  ,,  detachment of 28, 32
  ,,  views on the theory of government 32–34, 36
Cyneas 93

## INDEX

D'Annunzio 9
D'Aramont, see de Luetz
d'Aubigné 86
de Forest, Seigneur 42
de la Taille, Jean 98
de Luetz, Gabriel, Seigneur d'Aramont 55
Dennington 1
*De pace et bello*, occasion of dialogue 13
,, ,, authorship of 14–16
,, ,, significance of 20–24
,, ,, contents see Chapter I *passim*
de Roquelaure 72
De Serres 40
Design, Grand 91
,, ,, see Chapters IV and V *passim*
,, ,, alleged nature of Sully's 74, 75
Dijon 56
Divine Right of Kings 31
Doneau, education of 32, 39
,, views on the theory of government 32, 36
Duaren, on simplicity of Roman Law 27, 31
,, views of, on theory of government 31
,, Gallicanism of 31

Elizabeth, Queen of England 77–78, 81–83, 91
English Common Law 28
Erasmus 46
Estienne, Henri (1531–1598) 39, 40
Eugenius (IV), Gabriel Condulmero, Pope 3

Feminine sex, mystical appeal of 54, 56
Figgis, Dr J. N. (the late) 26, 31
France, Postel's views on 49–51
Francis (I), king of France 39, 41–42
Francis (II), king of France 37, 39, 66
Franco-British Agreement (1603) 80
*Franco-Gallia* 30, 35, 37, 86
Francowitz Mathias (Flaccus Illyricus) 40, 53
Franks, the 29

Germany 63, 81, 88, 95, 103
Giles, Peter 42, 55
Godfrey, Denys, *Consuetudines Parisienses* etc. 27
,, definitions of feudal terms 27

Godsalve, Thomas (of Norwich and Lichfield) 1
Gomer, Gomerites 49
Gospels, their teaching the application of principles to specific circumstances 21–22
Gothein 62
Gresham 104
Gronovius 92
Grotius, Hugo 48, 91, 92
Guise, the House of 37, 66
Gwynn 80

Halle, Treaty of 89
Hapsburg, House of 78–89, 102
Hatfield Papers 83
Henry (IV), king of France 28, 65, 66, 68, 73, 91, 97, 102, Chapter IV *passim*
,, right to the throne 33
Herbst, see Operinus
Hesse, Landgrave of 73
Hotman, *Antitribonian* 26
,, constitutionalism of 30
,, *Franco-Gallia* of 30, 35, 37, 86
House, Colonel 93
Hubbard, Peter 1
Huguenot political theory 37, 86

Ignatius, Patriarch 57
Illyricus, Flaccus, see Francowitz, Mathias
Inge, Dr W. R. 54
Ingolstadt, Otto Henry's Library 59
Italian theories of government 30

James (I), (VI), king of England and Scotland 79–85
James, Montagu Rhodes (Provost of Eton) 1
Japheth 49
Jeannin 68
Jesuits, the 39, 44–45, 51, 58, 80
Joanna, the New Eve 53–54, 56, 59
John of Salisbury 20
John (II), king of Castille 3

*La Satire Ménippée* 87
League of Nations 38, 65, 91, 101–103
L'Écluse des Loges, Abbé de 72
Lejay 58
Le Laboureur 71
*Le Nouveau Cynée* 86, Chap. V *passim*
Letus, Pomponius 10–11
Linacre, Thomas 1
Louis (XI), king of France 28
Louis (XIV), king of France 28
Luther, Martin 40, 96

## INDEX

Machiavelli 30, 69, 91
Maes 47, 52, 59
Maitland, F. W. 26
Marlowe, Christopher 93
Mathias, King of Hungary 5
Medici, Catharine de 30, 60
Melanchthon 40
Meredinaeus, Moses 57
Mirandola, Pico della 46
Montils-les-Jours, ordinance of 27

Neo-Platonism 7, 9
Non-resistance, Bishop Roderick's views on 23
,, the duty personal not corporate 22, 23

*Oechonomies Royales* 66, 69–72, 104
Operinus (Herbst) 57
Orange, Prince of 73
Oresme, Nicholas 104
Ostend, defence of 82
Oxford, Regius Professorship of Civil Law at 35

Papacy, policy of, in Europe and the Near East in XV century, *see* under Popes Pius II and Paul II
,, utilisation of "publicity" methods 6
Paris, printers at 30
,, School of Law 35
Parker, Matthew, Archbishop 1
Pastor, defence of Pope Paul II 4
Paternoster, the 47
Paul (II), Pope Pietro Barbo 1, 2, 25
,, accession 3
,, policy contrasted with that of Pius II 4–6
,, attitude towards contemporary movements 9
Paul (IV), Pope (Caraffa) 59
Petrarch, MS. of Plato 8
,, antiquarianism of 9
Pfister, Charles 84
*Philaster* 87
Philosophy, mediaeval 7–9
Piadena, Bartolomeo Sacchi da (Platina) 9–11, and Chapter I *passim*
,, behaviour in prison 11–13
,, lives of the Popes 12
,, librarianship at the Vatican 12
,, views of 16–18
Piccolomini, Aeneas Sylvius, *see* Pope Pius II

Piracy 95
Pius (II), Pope, Aeneas Sylvius Piccolomini, lawlessness after his death 3
,, policy contrasted with that of Paul II 4–6
Platina, *see* under Piadena, Bartolomeo Sacchi da
Plato 7, 8, 23
Plethon, Gemistos 8, 9
Podiebrad, George, King of Bohemia 5
Pole, Cardinal 58
Politiques, the 37
Pollard, Professor 26
Postel, William, *see* Chapter III *passim*, 86
,, constitutionalism of 30
,, scholarship of 39
,, appreciations of his life work 39–40, 61–64
,, views on Protestantism 43
,, views on Christian unity 44, 47
,, dismissal from Society of Jesus 45
,, his obsession as to the duality of nature 46
,, views on World Unity and France 48
,, views on the position of France 49
,, imprisoned 52, 59
,, works placed on the Index 58
,, epitaph on 61
Poyet, the Chancellor 42
Prerogative, *see* Chapter II *passim*
,, Ship Money Case 32
,, teaching of the French "civilians" on 37
Pyrrhus, King 93

Rabelais 39
Ramé 61
Reformation, excesses of 54
Renaissance, effect of, on Europe 2
,, contrasted with conciliar movement 6
,, Christian and pagan 7–9
,, typical reasoning of 20
,, French 65
Responsibility of kingship 30, 35
Reuchlin 46
Richelieu, Cardinal 69
Right of defence against aggression argued by Platina 17
Rodericus Sancius of Arevalo, *see* Chapter I *passim*
,, career of 3
,, argument of 18–25

## INDEX

Rodericus Sancius, *Speculum humanae vitae* of 20, 30
,, views on monarchy 30
Roman Law, *see* Chapter II *passim*
,, revived study of, effects on Europe 26
,, simplicity of 27
,, and monarchical theory 27
,, and the theory of numbers 46
Ronsard 39, 66
Rousseau 65

St Barbe, College of 41, 44
St Bartholomew, massacre of 67
Sainte-Beuve 71
St James, Pseudo-Gospel of, 55
St Martin, Paris, Monastery of 59-60
Saint Simonism 54
Salic Law 30, 33, 37
Sanctity of human life argued by Platina 16, 17
Sanseverini family and Piero (Pomponius Letus) 10
Scaliger, Joseph 60, 62
Scandinavian Powers 77
Seize, the 35, 37, 68
Sellinge, Prior of Christ Church, Canterbury 1
Seneca, quoted 31
Severus, Alexander, the Emperor 97
Ship Money Case 32
Silver, effect on European exchange of 2
Sixtus IV, Pope (Francesco della Rovere) 12
Smuts, General 101
Soleyman the Magnificent 55
Sorbonne, College of the 41
Southcott, Joanna 54
Spens, Will 23

*Studia Sinaitica* 55
Sully, *see* Chapter IV *passim*, 103
,, life 66
,, character 67
,, marriage 71
,, visit to Queen Elizabeth 77, 82-83
,, visit to King James I and VI 79, 83
,, motives in writing 87-90
Suso, Henry 54
Sutcliffe 40
Syriac studies 57

Tilley, Mr A. A. 71
Treitschke, Heinrich von, his *Politik* 20
Trent, Council of 9, 47
*Tribonian* 33
Turkish factor in Europe 4-6, 15, 48 55, 103

Ulpian 32, 33, 35
United States of America 63, 102
Utraquism 5

Vairani 1
Vatican, Library of 1, 12
Venice, Republic of and Cujas 33
,, City of 42, 52, 57, 58, 99
Vervins, Treaty of 88
Vienna, Congress of 38
,, City of 58-59
Vienne, Council of 48
Villebon, Château de 69-72
*Vindiciae contra tyrannos* 37, 86

War, educative force of 19
,, capable of right usage 21
"Weltmacht oder Niedergang" 20
Wheaton v
Widmanstadt 57-58